NELSON'S SPYGLASS

NELSON'S SPYGLASS

101 Curious Objects from British History

Sophie Campbell

First published 2016

The History Press
The Mill, Brimscombe Port
Stroud, Gloucestershire, GL5 2QG
www.thehistorypress.co.uk

British Library Cataloguing in Publication Data.
A catalogue record for this book is available from the British Library.

ISBN 978 0 7509 7003 7

Typesetting and origination by The History Press
Printed by IMAK.

Contents

ONE

Roman votive objects

These clay or metal body parts from 199 BC to AD 500 may look like novelties, but for the people who commissioned them they were were hugely significant. If you were suffering ill health, this was a way of begging the gods for help – or, for the lucky ones, thanking them for a cure. Each object, from two apparently healthy scalps to a slender foot in a sandal, is a window on the personal preoccupations of the distant past, perhaps representing broken limbs, hair loss or crippling headaches. This terracotta figure of a pregnant woman, discovered in Suffolk, holds her hands protectively over her belly, no doubt hoping for the safe delivery of her child.

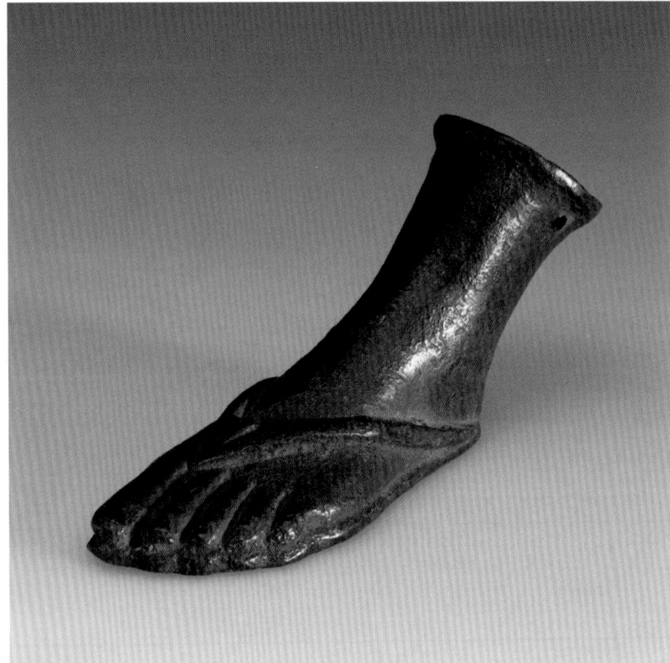

TWO

An Anglo-Saxon warrior's bandage

Headaches, fractures, haemorrhoids… the Anglo-Saxons had them too, along with picturesque cures such as spit, snails and birds' blood. Their medicine was a stew of folklore, herbal cures, fragments of classical knowledge, faith and superstition. This damaged limb from between AD 500 and AD 1,000 was found complete with copper 'bandage', the replica of which shows leaves packed next to the wound like a dressing. This is an exact copy of that bandage. Three or four plants then found in this country had limited antimicrobial properties. Stephanie Paul's essay on Old English medicine (herlid.org.uk) quotes this charm to be sung over a fallen warrior: 'For the wounds I have bound on the best of battle-bandages, so that the wounds may not burn or burst, Nor expand, nor multiply, nor skip about, Nor wound grow, nor lesion deepen; But to him (I) myself held out a cup of health, Nor may it pain you more than earth hurts earth.'

THREE

The Winchester Psalter

This exquisitely terrifying image from around AD 1150 is one of thirty-eight plates in the sumptuous Winchester (or St Swithun's) Psalter, commissioned by Henry of Blois in the mid-twelfth century. Henry was the younger brother of King Stephen and Abbot of Glastonbury from 1126. He was also one of the wealthiest men in England and the psalter was probably made for him – or possibly for a woman, as richly decorated psalters often were – by the scribes and limners of Winchester's cathedral priory. This shows the 'Harrowing of Hell', when Christ enters Hell after his crucifixion but before his ascent to Heaven. An angel unlocks the red door restraining a melee of humans and devils: look carefully to find two naked kings and a naked queen, all wearing tiny golden crowns.

FOUR

The Beowulf manuscript

'Listen!' begins the poem Beowulf, as it sets out to tell in verse the story of a Scandinavian warrior and his many travails. It may have existed in oral form long before two English scribes set it down on parchment around the year AD 1000, probably during the reign of Æthelred the Unready. That we have it at all is down to the Tudor antiquarian Laurence Nowell (hence 'Nowell Codex'), the tutor of Edward de Vere, who was thought by some to be the 'real Shakespeare'. Later it became part of the largest private collection in history, owned by the Cambridgeshire bibliophile Sir Robert Cotton, surviving confiscation by King Charles I and a catastrophic fire in 1731, 100 years after Cotton's death. This fragile and decomposing fragment is the only surviving copy of the poem.

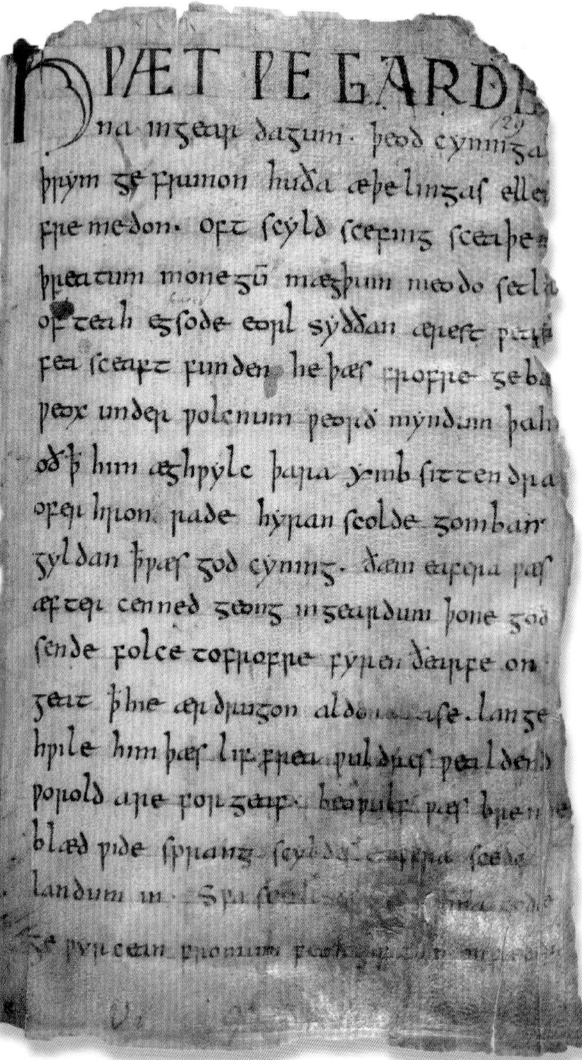

BRITANNIA
Saxonica.
Scala Milliarium
NOR-
HYMBRA
EAST
ENGLAS
FOLK
SEAXNA
CORNPEALLAS
SCYRE
John Sturt sculp

FIVE

Seal from the Article of the Barons

It seems miraculous that a beeswax seal could survive for 800 years, and this one is hugely significant. In June 1215 it was affixed to the Articles of the Barons – effectively the prototype for Magna Carta, the 'Great Charter', so called to distinguish it from a smaller treaty published simultaneously – which set out to limit the power of King John. John's figure, on horseback, is shown here on the reverse of the seal. Alongside is one of the British Library's two iterations of Magna Carta, written in ink made from iron-gall, or iron sulphate dissolved in acid made from the growths on oak trees. The only other 1215 charters in existence are at Lincoln Castle and Salisbury Cathedral.

SIX

Edward the Confessor's tomb

Edward the Confessor, the penultimate Anglo-Saxon king, shown here with book in hand, spent a tenth of the country's wealth building Westminster Abbey in the Romanesque cruciform (cross-shaped) style. He died as it was completed, and was canonized a century later. A cult grew up around his remains. He was canonised a century later and this print shows the thirteenth-century shrine built in his honour by King Henry III, whose patron saint he was: Henry III even named his son after the saint. Here, blind pilgrims wait to crawl into the niches and leave offerings, watched over by the saint himself, holding his famous ring. Henry III is buried in the Confessor's original coffin: he kept it when he 'translated' the saint's body to the new shrine.

SEVEN

Richard II's skull

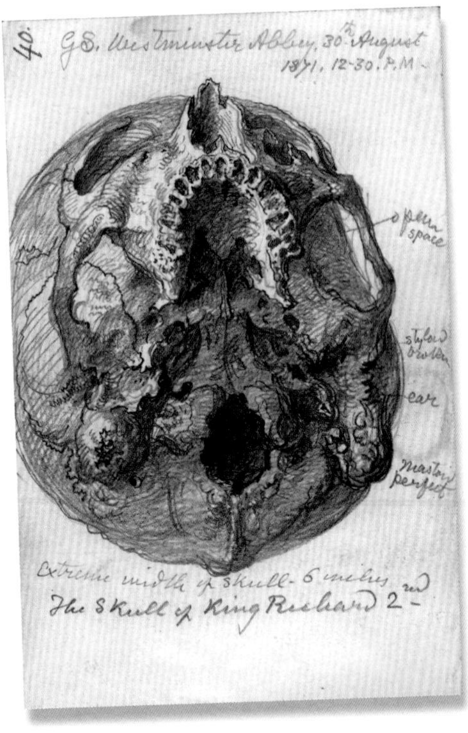

In 2010, an National Portrait Gallery archivist cataloguing the extensive papers of its first Director, Sir George Scharf, came across a small cardboard cigarette box. A careful copperplate hand had added '31st August 1871, Westminster Abbey, GS'. Inside lay scraps of wood, strips of leather and fragments of a purplish fabric. A cross-reference with the Director's diary then revealed something extraordinary. There, in matter-of-fact prose, Scharf had recorded the exhumation of King Richard II. 'I looked down into the grave,' he wrote. 'The skull of Richard I had in my hand and pressed to my lips.' An even closer encounter with the king awaited, for 'a small spongy compact substance (like a patella in shape) came from inside the [king's] skull'. It was 'very light; it had no taste nor smell'. The bones were 'quite dry and not at all musty'. Scharf also held Anne of Bohemia's skull, 'much smaller and lighter'. Anne was Richard II's first wife; she died of the plague in 1394, and the pair were buried together on Richard's decease. A check of the Director's sketchbooks also revealed this extraordinary and detailed sketch of Richard II's skull. The wood in the cigarette box most probably came from Richard's coffin; the fragments may come from a brown leather glove (which Scharf also drew), and from either the king's shoes or from his scabbard. By the time he drew this sketch, Scharf, an avid diarist and historian, had already attended the exhumations of Edward VI, Henry VII, James I and Elizabeth of York (in 1869). He was to attend the exhumation of Henry III in November 1871. Today, the relics from Sir George Scharf's cigarette box are the oldest items in the Gallery's archive.

EIGHT

Thomas Norton's Ordinal of Alchemy

This charming page from Thomas Norton's instruction book for alchemists, circa 1477, shows not only his apprentices stoking the fires, but the first known image of a scientific balance. The glass box stops the wind skewing the reading. Norton was esquire of the body to Edward IV and his book, produced in Bristol, also showed how to produce the 'Philosopher's Stone', a healing elixir that granted eternal life and turned base metals into gold. However, as Rosemary Guiley reveals in her *Encyclopedia of Magic and Alchemy*, on both occasions Norton managed to make the 'Great Red Elixir'.

NINE

Saint Thomas Becket's stone

The murder of Thomas Becket, Archbishop of Canterbury, inside his own cathedral and at the apparent behest of his former friend King Henry II, rocked Christian Europe. According to John Morris's *Life*, the first sword blow glanced from Becket's head. The second brought him to his knees, his head resting on this stone. Richard de Brito's third and fourth blows were so violent that his sword shattered. Hugh of Horsea then 'drew the brains from the wound and scattered them on the pavement … [the crown of the skull being] attached only by the skin of the forehead.' This stone thus represents the moment of England's most famous martyrdom. Relic hunters immediately soaked clothes and fabrics in his blood and gathered his brains up into a cup. Miracles duly followed and his reputation as a revered figure in British history was firmly established.

TEN

Black Death crosses

London has suffered plagues throughout its history, but the Black Death of the mid-1300s was on a different scale. These homemade metal crosses, found in a London cemetery, were a pitiful defence against the rampaging *Yersinia pestis* that would eventually kill as many as 200 million people across Europe. Crosses are often linked with plague, including 'trading crosses' erected so victims could trade without passing on infection. Three centuries later, afflicted households in the 1660s were 'marked with a red cross of a foot long in the middle of the door, evident to be seen, and with these usual printed words, that is to say, "Lord, have mercy upon us," to be set close over the same'.

ELEVEN

The Lindisfarne Gospels

Lindisfarne Priory, on remote Holy Island off the Northumberland coast, was not remote enough to avoid the Vikings. It was the first place in England to be attacked in June 793. The invaders 'miserably ravaged and pillaged everything; they trod the holy things under their polluted feet, they dug down the altars, and plundered all the treasures of the church.' But they didn't get this, the greatest treasure of all. The manuscript known as the Lindisfarne Gospels was written and illuminated over twenty years (from AD 698 to AD 721) by one man, according to its curators at the British Library. Eadfrith, Bishop of Lindisfarne, wrote his gospels for 'God and St Cuthbert' and put them between covers later adorned with glorious gold, silver-gilt and precious stones (since stripped away).

TWELVE

A penitent's belt

This painful-looking leather and iron belt, with its metal teeth, would have been tightened around the thigh of a religious penitent in order to achieve mortification of the flesh and therefore forgiveness from God. The practice was prevalent during the terrifying centuries of war, famine and plague that dominated Europe in the Middle Ages. Other devices included cilices, or hair shirts, and flagellation whips. The second set of spiked bands was worn tight around the ankles, cutting into the flesh. The word penitent is derived from the Latin *paean*, meaning praise, in this case meaning the suffering of the user offered as a sacrifice to God. Cilices comes from the Latin root *cicatrix*, 'scar'. Fans of Dan Brown's books may remember that the assassin in his *Da Vinci Code* wears just such a belt around his thigh.

THIRTEEN

Chaucer's grave

Relatives of Geoffrey Chaucer, fourteenth-century courtier, customs comptroller and writer of the first Middle English bestseller, *The Canterbury Tales*, never saw this elegant monument in Westminster Abbey. It was erected 150 years after his death by the Tudor writer Nicholas Brigham, at a time when there were still eighty editions of the *Tales* in circulation; it has never gone out of print. Chaucer's star waned with that of his political patron, John of Gaunt, and his original gravestone was later sawn up and used to fill in the Abbey floor when the poet Dryden was buried. But he's buried here, and other writers in English wanted to be so too: today they fill the South Transept, giving it its nickname, 'Poets' Corner'.

FOURTEEN

Leper's begging bowl

The contagious skin and nerve disease leprosy reached England as early as the fourth century AD. According to Historic England, the city of Winchester had a leper hospital long before the Norman Conquest. In the marginal image you see here, from around AD 1400, the leper is facially disfigured, with a bell to signify he is unclean. The idea of corruption and decay had moral and physical implications, and people avoided sufferers. These are copies of lepers' begging bowls: their long handles allowed passers-by to salve their consciences with a donation without getting too close.

FIFTEEN

Christopher Wren's Urn

Sitting quietly in the north aisle of the Lady Chapel, near Elizabeth I's tomb, Westminster Abbey is a decorative urn containing the supposed remains of the Princes in the Tower. The bones were discovered in 1674 under a staircase at the Tower of London, and Charles II ordered them brought to the Abbey. There the bones were interred in a white marble sarcophagus, made by Sir Christopher Wren. The inscription is in Latin, but the Abbey's translation runs thus: 'Here lie the relics of Edward V, King of England, and Richard, Duke of York. These brothers being confined in the Tower of London, and there stifled with pillows, were privately and meanly buried, by the order of their perfidious uncle Richard the Usurper; whose bones, long enquired after and wished for, after 191 years in the rubbish of the stairs (those lately leading to the Chapel of the White Tower) were on the 17th day of July 1674, by undoubted proofs discovered, being buried deep in that place. Charles II, a most compassionate prince, pitying their severe fate, ordered these unhappy Princes to be laid amongst the monuments of their predecessors, 1678, in the 30th year of his reign.'

SIXTEEN

Henry V's instructions

King Henry V wrote this letter to an unknown recipient a few years after the Battle of Agincourt. It requests a strong guard be set for 'alle the remanant of my prisoners of France, and also for the King of Scoteland [James I of Scotland, captured at sea on his way to France in 1406]'. This was because, as the letter continues, the king had been 'secretly enfourmed [secretly informed]' that plans were underway for 'the havyng awey specialy of the Duc of Orlians and also of the King' – a prison break! Charles of Orléans was captured at Agincourt after he unfortunately became wedged under a giant pile of corpses. He was to spend the next twenty-four years in various English prisons before being ransomed. At the time this letter was written he was at Pontefract Castle, as this letter shows: 'I wolle [will] that the Duc of Orliance be kept st[i]lle with the castil of Pontfret.'

SEVENTEEN

The Duke of Bedford's Hours

This portrait of John of Lancaster with St George captures the likeness of a man with a strange claim to fame – he was responsible for the trial and execution of Joan of Arc. John was the 1st Duke of Bedford and Henry V's brother; when Henry died, the Duke acted as regent for his nephew, Henry VI, focusing on the French wars, whilst his brother Humphrey protected England. But the French campaign suffered a setback: the arrival of the Maid of Orleans. The Duke had her burnt at the stake. He commissioned this manuscript from the Bedford Master in France as a wedding present for his future wife Anne (who sadly died of the plague in 1432). Just before her death, the pair presented the book to the young English king as a Christmas present.

EIGHTEEN

Henry VII's touch-pieces

For centuries people thought the monarch, as God's representative on earth, could cure scrofula at a touch (hence 'the King's Evil'. The disease caused swelling of the neck accompanied by blood and pus. Sometimes the king would indeed touch a sufferer, but no doubt he preferred to touch a coin – or by the time of Queen Anne, a lodestone – for the supplicant in turn to touch or even to wear. Shakespeare refers to men with 'a golden stamp about their necks' in *Macbeth*. The coins here bear Henry VIII's initials, a Tudor rose and his coat of arms emblazoned on a ship, with St George killing the dragon on the reverse. He actually touched the pierced coin, but the practice was finally ended by the practical George I, the first Hanoverian monarch.

NINETEEN

Henry VIII's Admission

King Henry VIII started life as a devout younger brother, headed for the Church, not the throne. This handsome deed admits him, as Prince of Wales, to the Order of the Most Holy Trinity and of the Captives. The twelfth-century priest St John de Matha founded the Order and bought back enslaved Christians from their Muslim captors in the Maghreb (although his Order happily ransomed slaves of all religions and nationalities). The Order reached England with the returning Crusaders, incorporating the royal arms into its red, white and blue cross. Henry still shut them down at the Dissolution.

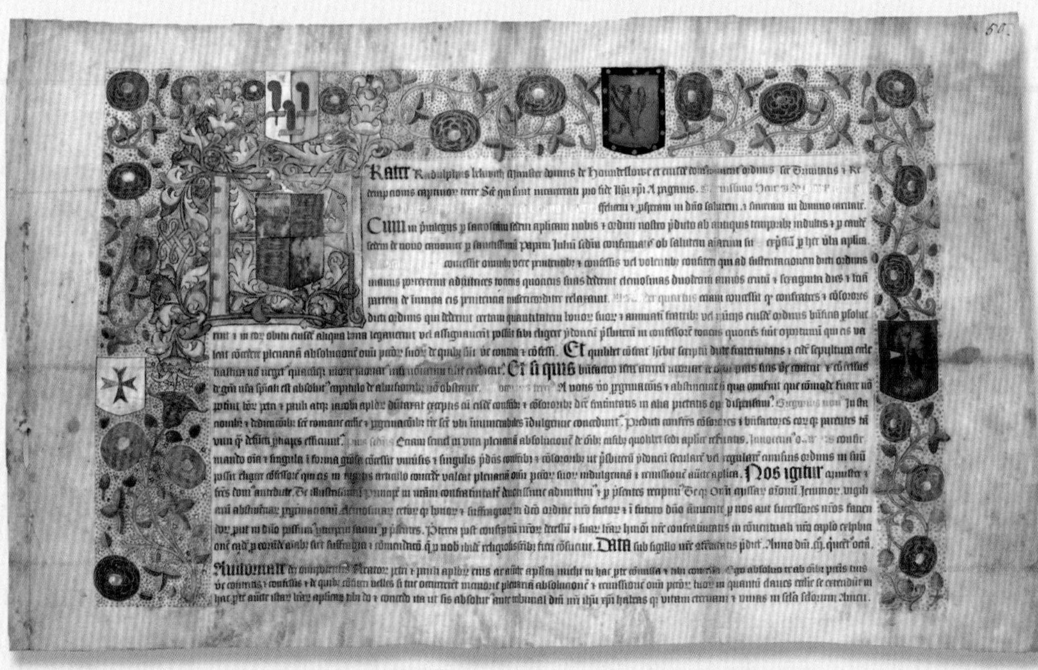

TWENTY

Henry VIII's prayer book

Here is Henry VIII, every inch the Renaissance king, depicted in his own prayer book, commissioned in 1540-42. He is dressed according to sumptuary laws in crimson velvet and cloth of gold. The other man is Will Somers, Henry's beloved jester, who may be wearing the very 'coate of grene clothe, with a hoode of the same' for which Henry paid 'John Malte, our Tillor (tailor)' on 28 June 1536. Somers ended up surviving four Tudor monarchs, though there were a few low spots: Henry VIII once threatened to kill him after he called the future Elizabeth I 'a bastard' and Anne Boleyn 'a ribald'. According to Robert Armin, an actor in Shakespeare's troupe, Somers once threw a bowl of milk at another jester to stop him hogging the court's attention.

TWENTY-ONE

Katherine of Aragon's announcement

Henry VIII's first wife is famous as a wronged queen, but she was highly educated and a more than competent regent when Henry was away fighting in France early in their marriage. This triumphant letter, written from Woburn Abbey in Bedfordshire, describes the 'grete victorye' over the Scots at the Battle of Flodden Field in 1513. It was hideously bloody by modern standards: the English lost 1,500 men, the Scots an appalling 10,000, including their king, James IV, who was slashed to death with English billhooks (effectively a knife on a giant stick, with a wickedly sharp hook on the side). The English also had cannon, which fired 2lb lumps of metal straight into the Scottish lines. After the battle Katherine was given James's ripped, bloodied surcoat: she has sent it to the king, she explains in the letter, to be turned into 'baners' (battle banners). She would have sent him the body too, she adds, 'but our Englisshem hertes wold not suffre it…'

Sir my lord Havard hath sent me a letter open to your grace within
oon of myn by the which ye shal see at length the grete victorye
that our lord hath sent your subgetts in your absence and for
this cause it is noo nede herin to troble your grace wt long
writing but to my thinking this batell hath bee to your grace
and al your reame the grettest honor that coulde bee and more
than ye shulde wyn al the crowne of ffrance thankes bee god
of it and i am sure your grace forgetteth not to doo this wch
shalbe cause to sende you many moo suche grete victoryes as
i trust he shal doo / my husband for hastynesse wt Rogecrosse i
coulde not sende your grace the pece of the king of Scotts cote
whiche John Glyn now bringeth in this your grace shal see
how i can kepe my promys sending you for your baners a kings
cote / i thought to sende hymself unto you but our englishemens
herts wold not suffre it / it shulde have been better for hym to
have been in peax than to have this rewarde / al that god
sendeth is for the best // my lord of Surrey my henry wolde fayne
knowe your pleasure in the buryeng of the king of Scotts body
for he hath written to me soo / with the next messanger your
grace pleasure may bee herin knowen / and wt this i make an
ende praying god to sende you home shortly for without this
noo joye here can bee accomplisshed / and for the same i pray
and now goo to our lady at Walsyngham that i promised soo
long agoo to see / at Woborne the xvi day of Septembre
I sende your grace herin a bille founde in a Scottysshemans purse of
suche things as the frenshe king sent to the said king of Scotts
to make warre agaynst you beseching you to sende mathewe hider
assone this messanger commeth to bringe me tydings from your grace

Your humble wif and
true servant

Katherine

My lord after my most humble recomendacions this shall be to gyve unto your grace
as I am most bownd my humble thanks for the gret payn and travell that your
grace doth take in steudyeng by your wysdome and gret dylygens howe to bryng
to pas honerably the gretyst welth that is possyble to com to any creator lyvyng
and in especyall remembryng howe wrechyd and unwrthy I am in comparyng
to his hyghnes / and for you I do knowe my self never to have deservyd by my desertes
that you shuld take this gret payn for me yet dayly of your goodnes I do perceyve
by all my frends and though that I hade not knowlege by them the dayly
proffe of your deds doth declare your words and wrytyng toward me to be
trewe nowe good my lord your dyscressyon may consyder as yet how lytel it
is in my power to recompence you but all onely with my good wyl the whiche
I assewer you that after this matter is brought to pas you shall fynd me
as I am bownd in the meane tym to owe you my servyse and then looke
what thyng in this world I can imagen to do you pleasor in you
shall fynd me the gladdyst woman in the world to do yt and next
unto the kyngs grace of one thyng I make you full promes to be assewryd
to have yt and that is my harty love unfaynydly deuryng my lyf
and beyng fully determynd with godds grace never to change thys
porpos I make anend of thys my rude and trewe meanyd letter
praying oure lord to send you moche increse of honor with long lyfe
wrytten with the hand of her that besechys your grace to except this letter
as prosydyng from one that is most bownd to be

Your humble and
obedient servant

anne boleyn

TWENTY-TWO

Anne Boleyn's thank-you note

Both writer and recipient of this neatly-penned letter would be dead within a decade. Anne Boleyn was writing to thank the powerful Cardinal Wolsey for promoting her marriage to the already-married king. 'My humble thanks for the gret payn and travell that your grace doth take…' she wrote, 'howe to bryng to pas honerably the gretyst welth that is possyble to come to any creatour lyvyng'. She promised him her future loyalty – until he failed to annul the king's first marriage and was arrested and stripped of his titles. Wolsey died en route to his trial for treachery. Anne lost her head six years later at the Tower.

Cardinal Wolsey.
From the original of Holbein, in the Collection at
Christ Church, Oxford.

TWENTY-THREE

Anne Boleyn's portrait of Henry VIII

This portrait of King Henry VIII, broad, blue-eyed and implacable, decorated *The Penitential and other Psalms* carried by Anne Boleyn to the scaffold. She gave the tiny volume to her lady-in-waiting and made a dignified speech recorded by historian John Stow: 'I beseech Jesu save my Sovereign and master the King, the most goodliest, and gentlest Prince that is, and long to reign over you, which words she spake with a smiling countenance: which done, she kneeled down on both her knees, and said, To Jesu Christ I commend my soul and with that word suddenly the hangman of Calais smote off her head at one stroke with a sword: her body with the head was buried in the choir of the Chapel in the Tower.' Her ladies carried her head and corpse into the chapel of St Peter ad Vincula, where she lies under the altar.

TWENTY-FOUR

Katherine Parr's needlework

Katherine Parr, 'KP', was the fashionable, devoutly Protestant last wife of Henry VIII. She was also a skilled needlewoman and embroidered this charming velvet book cover for her own copy of Petrarch. She probably made it after Henry's death, because his heraldic supporters (the English lion and the Richmond greyhound) are not supporting the shield below the crown. Instead, she has used her parents' arms and her own, including the writhing wyvern – or winged dragon – on the right, sewn in blue silk and gold cording.

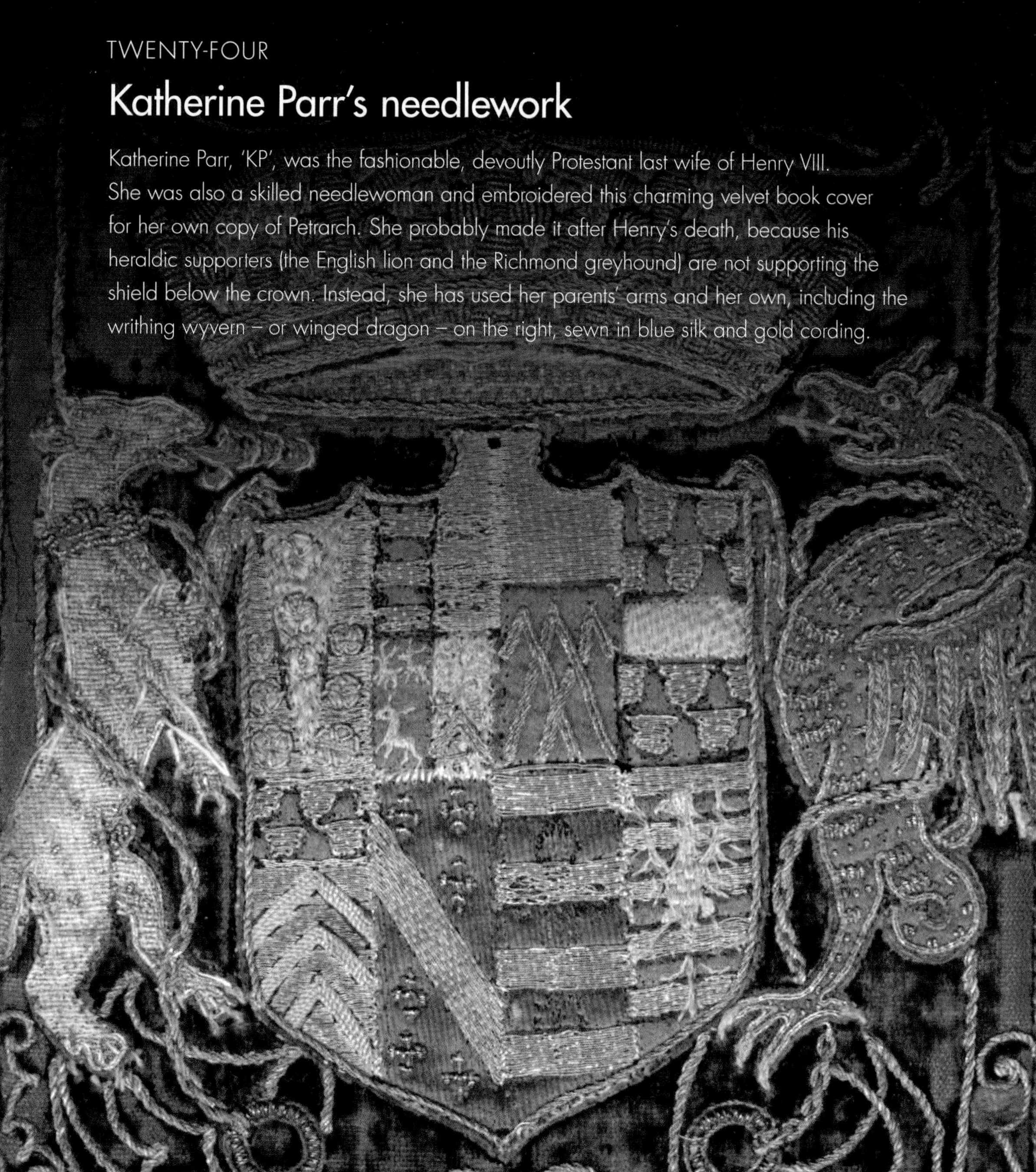

18. The L Mary my sister came to me to whestminster
wheare after salutacions she was called w^t my
counsel into a chambre, where was declared how
long i had suffered her masse ~~against my will~~
in hope of her reconciliation, and how now
being no hope, wich i perceiued by her lettres
except i saw some short amendement, i could not
beare it. She answerid that her soul was god
and her faith she wold not chaunge, nor dissemble
hir opinion w^t contrary doinges. It was said
constrained not her faith, but willed her not as a king to rule but
to obey, ~~or els~~ as a subiect. And that her exawmple might
breed to much inconuenience.

19 Themperours embassadour came w^t short messag
frome his master of warre, if i wold not
suffre his cosin the princesse to use hir
masse. To this was no aunswer giuen at
this time. ~~but the nex~~

20. The bis. of Caunterbury, London, ~~and~~ Rochester
did conclude to giue licence to sinne was sinne;
to suffre and winke at it for a time, might
be borne, so al hast possible might bee
used

TWENTY-FIVE

Edward VI's diary

The Protestant King Edward VI acceded aged nine, taking precedence over his Catholic sister, Mary. The writing in his diary, in recognizably modern English (he is perhaps the easiest of the Tudor monarchs to read) reveals their clash over the religious issues that were soon to rip the kingdom apart. 'The L[ady] Mary, my sister, came to me,' he wrote, 'where was declared how long I had suffered her masse in hope of her reconciliation, and how now being no hope, wich I perceiued by her lettres … I could not beare it. She answerid that her soul was God['s], and her faith she wold not chaung, nor dissemble [lie about] hir opinion with contrary doinges.' Mary would go on to martyr at least 300 Protestant subjects in her five short years on the throne.

TWENTY-SIX

Lady Jane Grey's orders

Lady Jane Grey wrote this letter (or rather, her secretary wrote it and she signed it) on 10 July 1553. She had just become queen. It was sent to William Parr, Marquis of Northampton. 'We ar entred into our rightfull possession of this kingdome, as by the last will of our sayd derest cousyn [Edward VI] … signed with his owne hande and sealed with the greate seale of this realme in his owne presence,' she writes. Then she gives her orders: for him to 'disturbe, repell and resist the fayned and vntrewe clayme [untrue claim] of the Lady Marye, bastard daughter of our great vunle Henry theight [Henry VIII] of famous memorye'. That is, to crush the bastard 'Bloody' Mary Tudor, and resist her attempts to seize the throne. It was signed at the 'Toure of London'. Lady Jane, who was just sixteen, was executed, having never again left the Tower, on 12 February 1554.

Jane the Quene

Right trusty and welbiloved we grete you well advertising you that where it hath pleased almighty god to call to his mercye out of this life our derest cousyn the king your late soveraigne lorde by reason wherof and suche ordonnance as the sayd late king did establishe in his lif tyme for the securitie and welthe of this realme we ar entred into our rightfull possession of this kingdome as by the last will of our sayd derest cousyn our late progenitor and other severall instrumentes to that effect signed with his owne hande and sealed with the greate seale of this realme in his owne presence wherunto the nobles of this realme for the most parte and all our counsell and judges with the mayor and aldermen of our citie of London and dyverse other grave personages of this our realme of England have also subscribed their names as by the same will and instrument it maye more evydently and playnly appere we therfore doo you to understande that by thordonnance and sufferance of the hevenly lorde and by the assent and consent of our sayd nobles and counsellors and others before specified we do this daye make our entrie into our Tower of London as rightfull Quene of this realme and have accordingly set furthe our proclamations to all our loving subjectes gyving them therby to understande their duetie of allegeaunce which they now owe unto us as more amplye by the same ye shall briefly perceive and understand nothing doubting right trusty and welbiloved but that ye will endevour yourself in all thinges to thuttermost of your power not only

TWENTY-SEVEN

Queen Elizabeth I's medal

Si Deus nobiscum, quis contra nos ('If God is with us, who can be against us?') reads the inscription on this gold medal, struck to give thanks for the recovery of Queen Elizabeth I from smallpox. She kept her life and her sight, unusually for the era, and for the rest of her days covered her scars with white face paint. The medal shows the queen's profile on one side and on the reverse a hand casting a snake into the flames; an allusion to St Paul, who miraculously survived the bite of a venomous serpent. Anne of Cleves also survived smallpox: her scars were one of the things hidden from Henry VIII in the famous Holbein painting which formed the basis of his agreeing to marry her.

POSVI · DEVM · ADIVTORVM · MEVM · 1572

TWENTY-EIGHT

Queen Elizabeth I's Bible

Bibles, their translation and printing, were contentious – dangerously so in the Tudor world. This 1568/9 Bishop's Bible, printed in London by Richard Lugge, was the second authorized version in English. It had royal assent, hence the wonderfully overblown frontispiece of Queen Elizabeth I being crowned by Justice and Mercy. Look for details such as the tiny hourglass used by the preacher to time his sermon, and the motto 'God save the queene' at the bottom. The Bishop's Bible had the initials of its episcopal translators on each chapter, and came with 124 full-page illustrations. It had to be revised shortly afterwards, partly because the Psalms proved impossible to sing. It is nicknamed the 'Treacle Bible' as the verse 'is there no balm in Gilead?' from Jeremiah 8:22 is rendered 'is there no treacle in Gilead?'

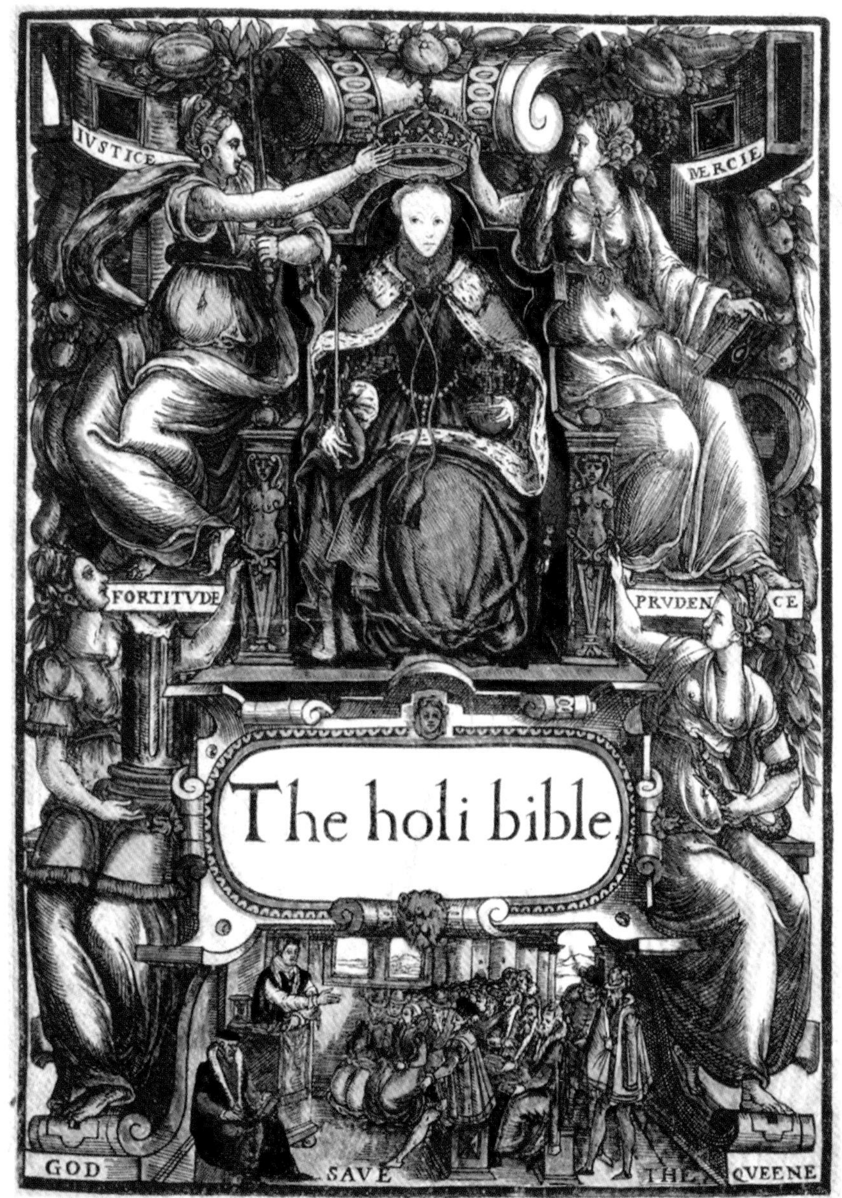
IVSTICE
MERCIE
FORTITVDE
PRVDEN CE
The holi bible.
GOD
SAVE
THE
QVEENE

TWENTY-NINE

John Dee's magical equipment

John Dee, mathematician, astronomer, astrologer and occultist, was tutor and magician to Queen Elizabeth I, who is shown observing one of his experiments in this nineteenth-century painting by Henry Gillard Glindoni. Dee's 'mystical objects' included this flat, dark Claude glass (used for divination) in a sharkskin case, used for divination, and the mysterious crystal – possibly a 'scrying mirror' for contacting the spirits – given to him, he said, by the Angel Uriel in 1582. Elizabeth trusted him, choosing her coronation date on his advice, but he became increasingly obsessed with magic and conversing with angels. He was even arrested by 'Bloody Mary' for casting the horoscopes of the royal family. Robert Cotton, the bibliophile, later found Dee's 'angel manuscripts' buried at the astronomer's house.

After my very harty comendations. I have receaved and shewd yr
lre signed by you and others of her Mats privie and
secret counsell. and settyng asyde my opinio concurryng wt
the tenor of your lre, I must deliver her Mats
answer resolut. she semeth to mislyke yt ye particularytes
of ye Scottish Queens lres war conteaned in the Judgment
but how so ever I allowed therof, and her Maty mislykyng
yet now I concluded wt her Maty, ther was no
remedy left to chang that and for ye prosecutyng
therof in deliveryng of ye evidece, hir pleasure is
that ther be no enlargment of hir cryme, but barly
declared for mayntenance of ye judgment, that she
allowed of Babyngtons wrytyng or lre. nether wold
she yt either by my L. Cobha. your self, or by any
other, any sharp speches be used in condemnation or reproch
of ye Scott. Queen. The only reason yt hir Maty alledgeth
is, that when any of hir frends or partisans, shall by this
oppe proceding, fynd hir in danger, for what may be attempted
to hir Mats danger of hir person in ye meane tyme
for ye form in ye Judgment, hir Maty is content it be kept, and so I
wrot to daye, but she will yt it be added in ye end, that
nevertheless such an extraordinary cryme, deserveth a further extraordinary
payne which is to be left to hir Maty and hir counsell
to consider of. Thus in hast I end, prayeng you to
comunicat this ever as much as you shall thynk mete, to ye rest
of hir Mats Counsell, and Judges. Haus after. W Burghley
Sept at night after ix of ye clok

THIRTY

William Cecil's instructions

'Burghley' says the signature scrawled at the bottom of this letter: you can feel the urgency as Elizabeth's spymaster Lord Burghley ties up the loose ends of the Babington Plot. Mary, the Catholic Queen of Scots, was accused of conspiring to kill her English cousin. Mary's trial is shown in this carefully annotated drawing: she was executed at the age of forty-four. This letter reveals the horrors to come for the accused plotters: Elizabeth I, wrote Burghley, thought that 'such an extraordynary cryme [as attempting to murder the queen] deserveth a furder extraordinary payne, which is to be left to hire Majesty and hir counsell to consider of.' The 'further pain' – the drawing and quartering of the first conspirators – caused such disgust that the second group of conspirators were allowed to die before they were drawn (their intestines drawn out) and quartered (cut into four sections).

THIRTY-ONE

Francis Drake's signature

Elizabeth I's famous Tilbury speech ('being resolved, in the midst and heat of the battle, to live and die amongst you all … I know I have the body of a weak, feeble woman; but I have the heart and stomach of a king, and of a king of England too, and think foul scorn that Parma or Spain, or any prince of Europe, should dare to invade the borders of my realm') was actually given after the defeat of the Spanish Armada. On 1 August 1588, her Council of War resolved to chase the defeated Spanish Armada 'vntill we haue cleared oure owne coaste'. The signatures on this resolution belong to Lord High Admiral Charles Howard, the commander of the fleet (and the man who persuaded Elizabeth I to sign Mary Queen of Scots' death warrant); the Queen's Champion George Clifford, the Earl of Cumberland, once described as 'the rudest Earll by reson of his northerly bringen up'; and Thomas Howard, Earl of Suffolk, who commanded the *Golden Lion* against the Armada and was knighted for his efforts the next day. The other marks are for Lord Sheffield; the famous Sir Francis Drake; Sir Edward Hoby; Vice-Admiral Sir John Hawkins, who designed the faster ships which won the battle; and Captain Thomas Fenner.

1. Augusti. 1588

We whose names are hereunder written have determined and agreede in counsaile to followe and pursue the Spanishe Fleete untill we have cleared oure owne coaste and broughte the Frithe weste of us. And then to returne backe againe aswell to revictuall oure shipps which stand in extreme scarsitie as alsoe to guard and defend oure owne coaste at home with further protestatione that if oure wante of victualls and munitione were supplied we wold ~~suppl~~ pursue them to the furthest that they durste have gone./

C. Howard George Coumbreland

T. Howard Edmonde Sheffeylde

Fra: Drake Edw. Hoby

John Hawkyns

Thomas Fenner

1° Augusti.
Determyned by the counsell
to returne from [illegible]
of the Frythe

THIRTY-TWO

Elizabeth I's present

In 1546, when Princess Elizabeth was twelve, she gave this little book to her father, Henry VIII, as a New Year's present. This was tactful: the book, entitled *Prayers or Mediations*, was by her stepmother. It was written in English and translated by Elizabeth into Latin, French and Italian. The binding, from the back cover, is crimson silk embroidered with gold and silver thread and coloured silks. The H stands for Henry, the K for Katharina or Katherine, and below is the lion of England; there are Tudor roses in the corners. The preface is believed to include the only surviving note from Elizabeth to her father.

THIRTY-THREE

A Tudor man's artificial arm

This iron arm, according to legend, belonged to a German knight who lost his real arm in a battle in 1503 and resourcefully asked his armourer to make him a replacement. It's a fine example of a Tudor trend sparked by the pioneering work of Ambroise Paré, surgeon to the French kings. Paré, a Huguenot, was in Paris during the St Bartholomew's Day Massacre: the king hid him in a cupboard to save his life. His work on the battlefield wrought amazing changes: wounds were no longer cauterised with boiling oil, for example. According to the National Center for Biotechnology Information, he designed mechanical limbs for the amputees he worked with. The legs had knees that could bend, and one of his mechanical hands was worn into battle by a French captain, who could hold and release his horse's reins with it.

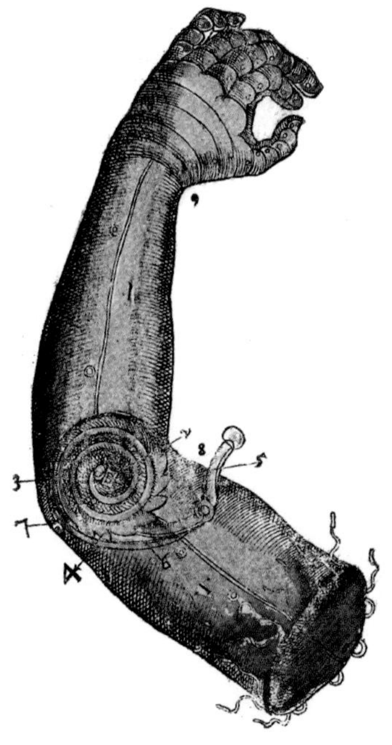

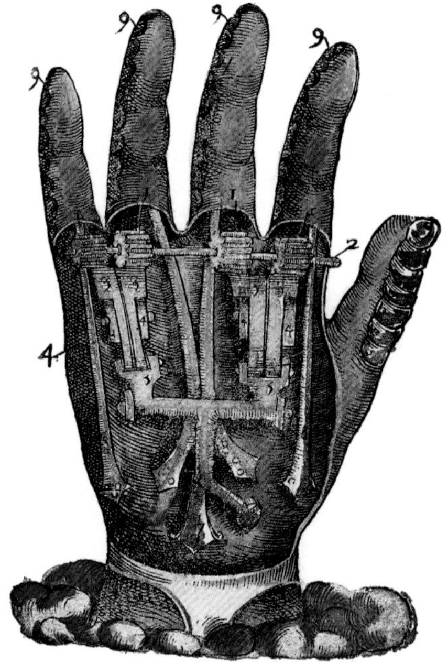

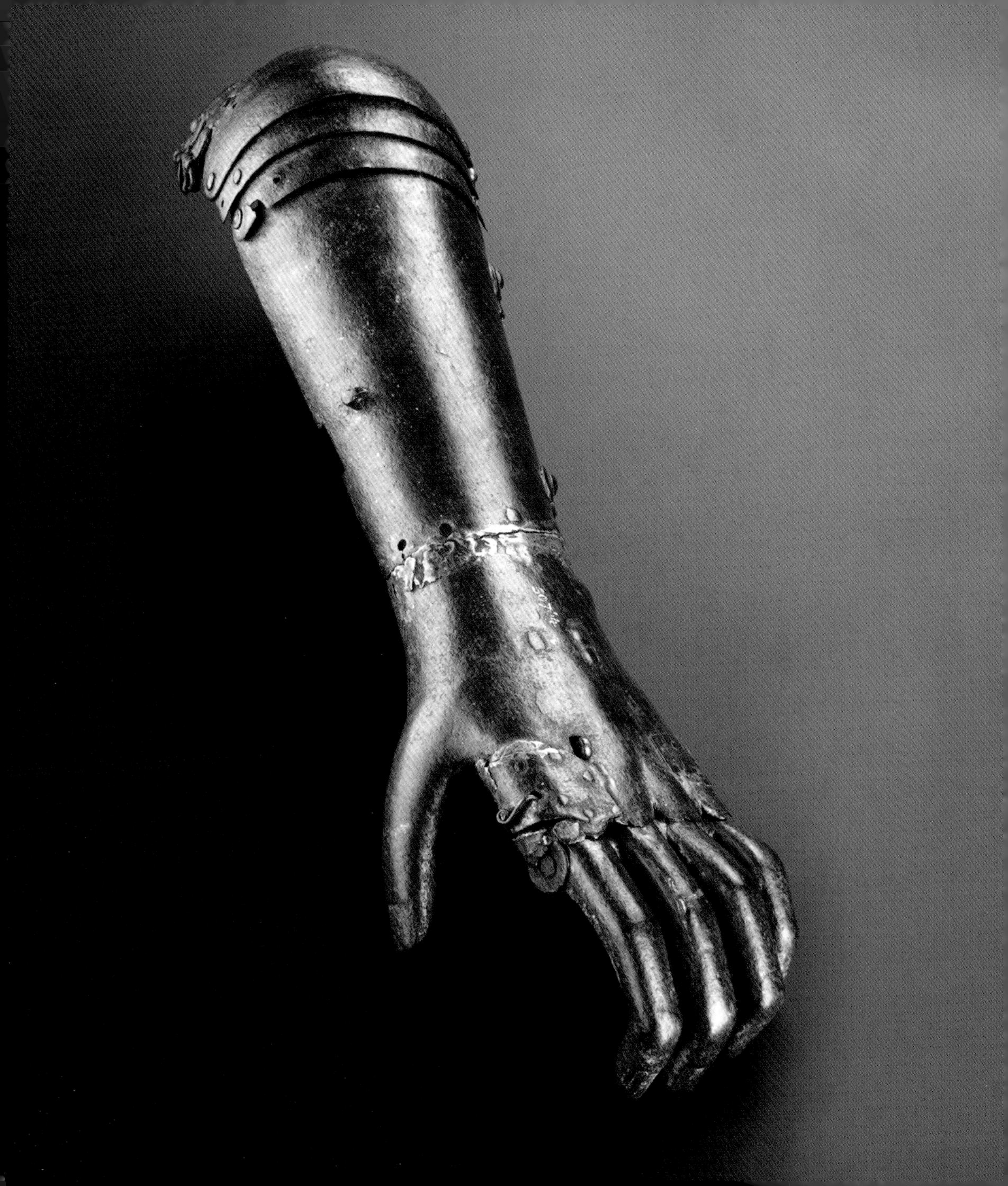

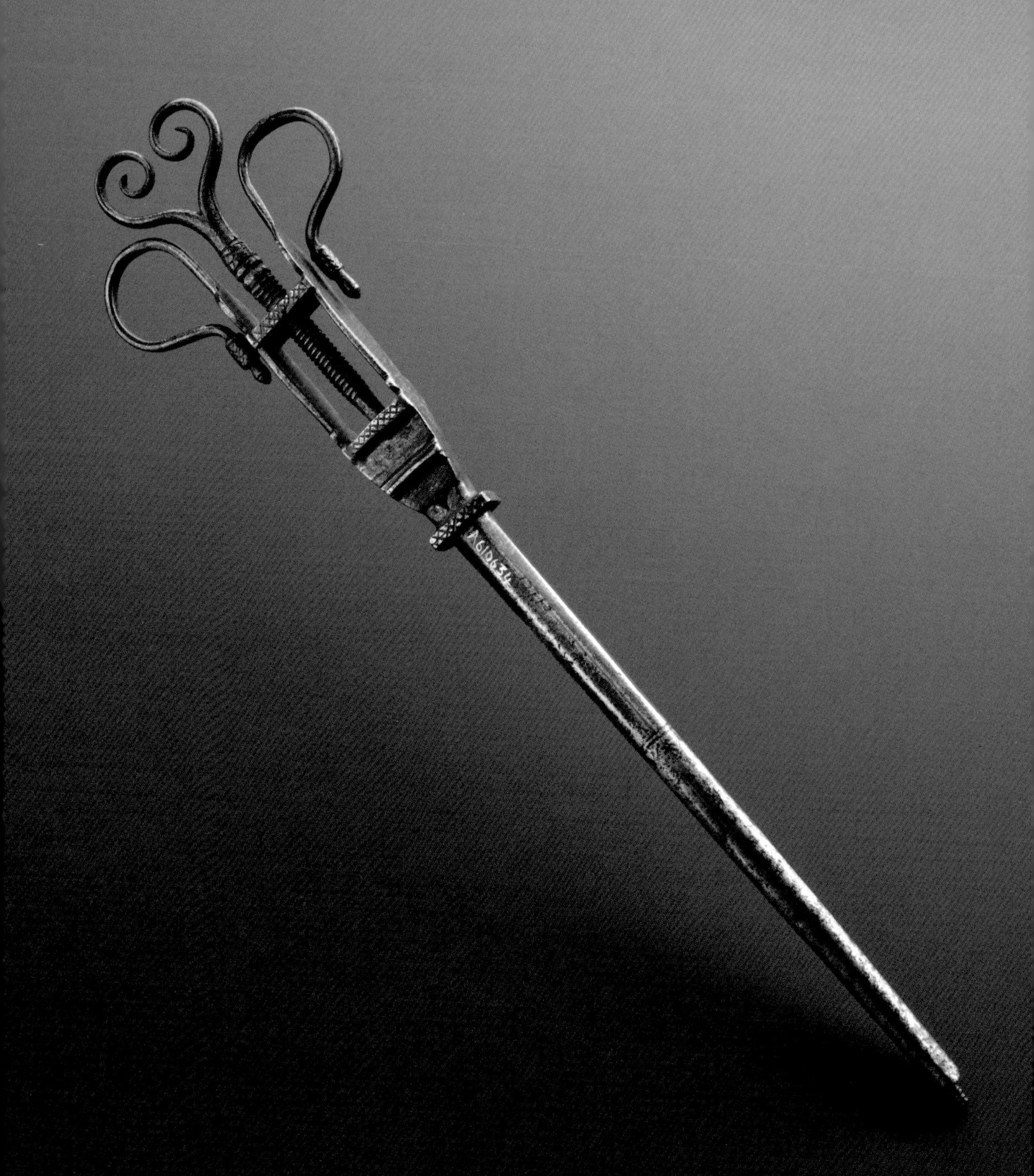
A616634

THIRTY-FOUR

A Tudor doctor's bullet extractor

As the very earliest firearms began to appear in the 1200s, battlefield injuries changed. Three centuries later, instruments like this one, made by an unknown European craftsman, were used to extract bullets from deep inside the body. Its hollow shaft was inserted into the wound, the central screw turned to pierce the embedded bullet, then the whole thing was withdrawn. The print shows a battlefield operation with the extractor deep in the wounded man's chest, as he is held down by a helper. In the background, battle continues to rage as artillerymen aim their weapons at rows of traditional pikemen.

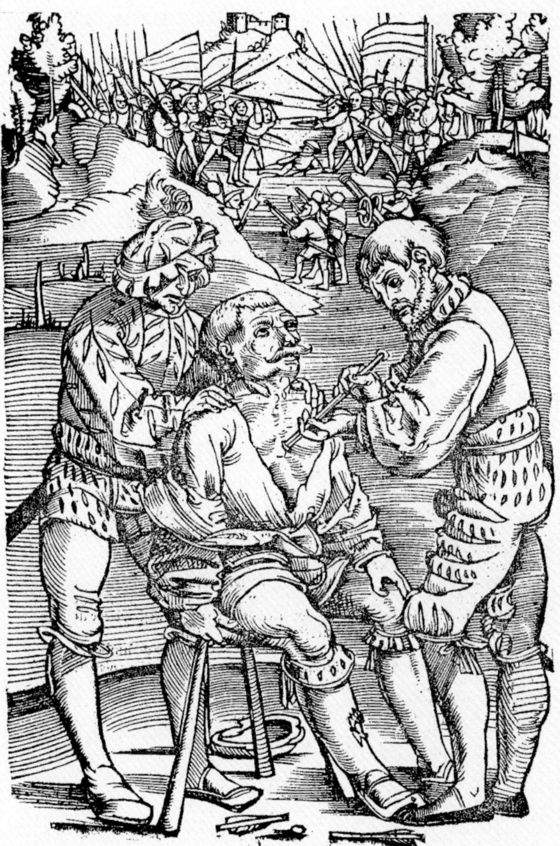

THIRTY-FIVE

Guy Fawkes's confession

Guy Fawkes, one of the Catholic plotters planning to blow up King James I and Parliament in 1605, was brutally tortured in the Tower of London. This is a facsimile of part of his confession and the samples of his signature taken before and after his torture show its shattering effect. He told his torturers that the plotters had considered approaching Sir Walter Raleigh to 'drawe' him into their conspiracy. The witnesses included Attorney General Sir Edward Coke (who had sent the 'vile viper' Raleigh to the Tower just over a year before); Sir William Wade, Lieutenant of the Tower, and Edward Forsett, part of the prosecution team who convicted the plotters. Their appalling deaths by hanging, drawing and quartering are vividly shown in this print. Mercifully, Fawkes himself was not drawn and quartered: he threw himself from the ladder at the gallows and broke his neck before the executioners could reach him.

B They five did meete at a Howse in the feilds, beyond St Clements Inn, where they did Confirr and Agree upon the Plott they ment to undertake, and put in Execucon. and there they tooke a solemne Oath and vowe, by all their force and Power to Execute the same, and of Secrecy not to Reveale anie of their fellowes, but to such as should be thought fitt persons to enter into that Accon; And in the same Howse they did receave the Sacrament of Gerrard the Jesuite to performe their vowe, and of secrecy as is aforesaid. But he saith that Gerrard was not acquainted wth their purpose

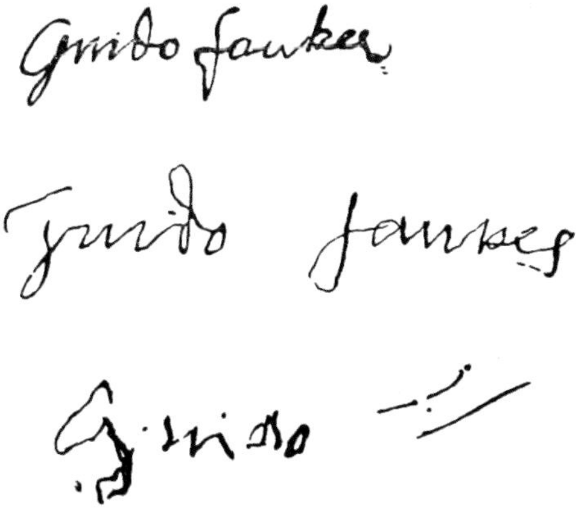

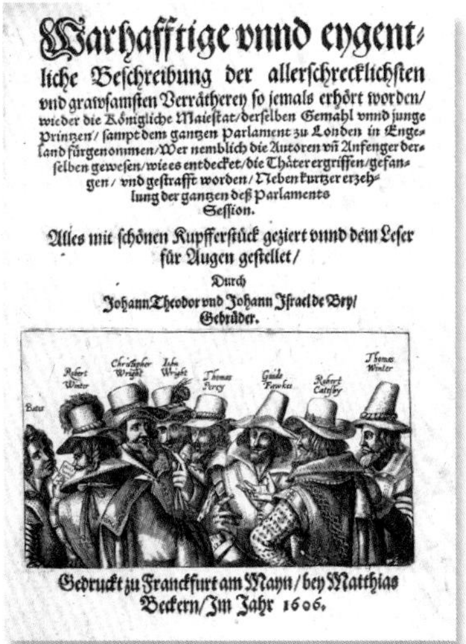

Warhafftige vnnd eygentliche Beschreibung der allerschrecklichsten vnd grawsamsten Verrätherey so jemals erhört worden/ wieder die Königliche Maiestat/derselben Gemahl vnnd junge Printzen/ sampt dem gantzen Parlament zu Londen in Engeland fürgenommen/Wer nemblich die Autoren vñ Anfenger derselben gewesen/wie es entdecket/die Thäter ergriffen/gefangen/ vnd gestrafft worden/ Neben kurtzer erzehlung der gantzen deß Parlaments Session.

Alles mit schönen Kupfferstück geziert vnnd dem Leser für Augen gestellet/

Durch

Johann Theodor vnd Johann Israel de Bry/ Gebrüder.

Gedruckt zu Franckfurt am Mayn/ bey Matthias Beckern/ Im Jahr 1606.

THIRTY-SIX

Pocahontas's buttons

These fine gold buttons may have been worn by Pocahontas, daughter of the paramount Powhatan chief in the new English colony of Virginia, when presented at the court of King James I. In 1616 she married the widower John Rolfe, who had introduced tobacco-growing to the new settlers, and came to England as Lady Rebecca Rolfe. She appeared at court, perhaps wearing the magnificent ensemble she is seen in here, and attended the masque. Rolfe family lore says the buttons and a pair of earrings were preserved from her stay. Such craftsmanship, not yet available in the American colony, indicates they were made in Europe.

THIRTY-SEVEN

Shakespeare's signature

On 10 March 1613, William Shakespeare bought an apartment in London. His signature, affixed to the mortgage for his new property in Blackfriars Gatehouse, just near the winter theatre used by the King's Men, is one of only six examples in existence. The playwright was by this time a prosperous businessman. Gatehouse and theatre were on the site of the Blackfriars Monastery, dissolved by Henry VIII. The house had a dark history: years before it was claimed the house 'hath sundry back doors and bye-ways, and many secret vaults and corners. It hath been in time past suspected and searched for papists…' Shakespeare himself never lived in the building, but left it to his family on his death. This deed was bought at auction by the Corporation of London in 1843, for the princely sum of £145.

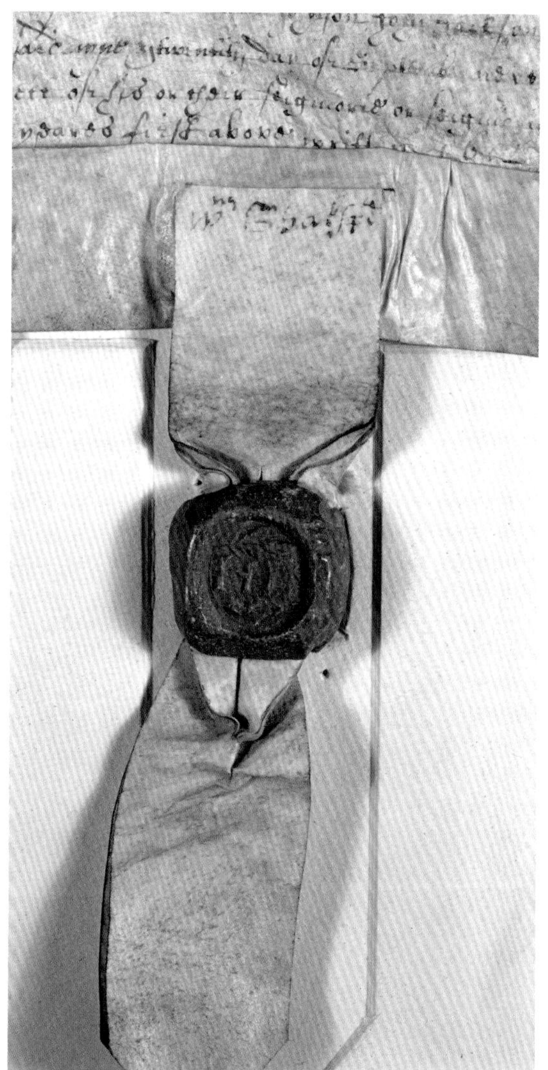

Sr. beinge Comanded by you to this
service, I thinke my selfe bound to ac=
quaint you with the good hand of God
towards you, and vs, wee marched yesterday
after the Kinge whoe went before vs
from Dauentree to Haurebrowe, and quar
tered about six miles from him, this day
wee marched towards him, Hee drew out
to meete vs. both Armies engaged, wee.
after 3 howres fight, very doubtfull
att last routed his Armie, killed and
tooke about 5000. very many officers
but of what quallitye wee yett know
not, wee tooke alsoe about 200. carrag
all hee had, and all his gunns, beinge
12. in number, whereof 2. were demi
canon, 2 demie Culveringes, and (I
thinke) the rest Sacres, wee pursued
enimie from three miles short of Ha°
to nine beyond, even to sight of Leic
whether the Kinge fled. Sr. this is non
other but the hand of God, and to him
aloane belongs the Glorie, wherein no
are to share with him. The Generall
served you with all faythfullnesse an
honor, and the best comendations I ca
give him is, that I dare say hee

attributes all to God, and would rather perish then assume to himselfe,
which is an honest, and a thriveinge way, and yett as much for bravery may
bee given to him in this action, as to a man. Honest men served you faythfully
in this action. Sr. they are trustye, I beseech you in the name of God not to
discourage them. I wish this action may begett thankfullnesse, and humilitye
in all that are concerned in itt, Hee that venters his life for the libertye of his
countrie, I wish hee trust God for the libertye of his conscience, and you
for the libertye hee fights for, In this hee rests who is

your most humble servant

Oliver Cromwell

June 14th 1645.
Haurebrowe.

THIRTY-EIGHT

Cromwell's announcement

This letter from Oliver Cromwell to William Lenthall, Speaker of the House of Commons, is precisely worded despite being dated 14 June 1645, the day of the Parliamentarian victory over King Charles I at Naseby. 'This day we marched towards [the King]…' he writes, 'Wee after 3 howers fight, very doubtful, att last routed his Armie, killed and tooke about 5000, very many officers, but of what quallitye wee yett know not.' The king fled to Leicester and Cromwell commended his victory to the Lord. 'This is non other but the hand of God,' he ends, 'to him aloane belongs the Glorie.' The defeat was the beginning of the end for Charles, who was executed in 1649.

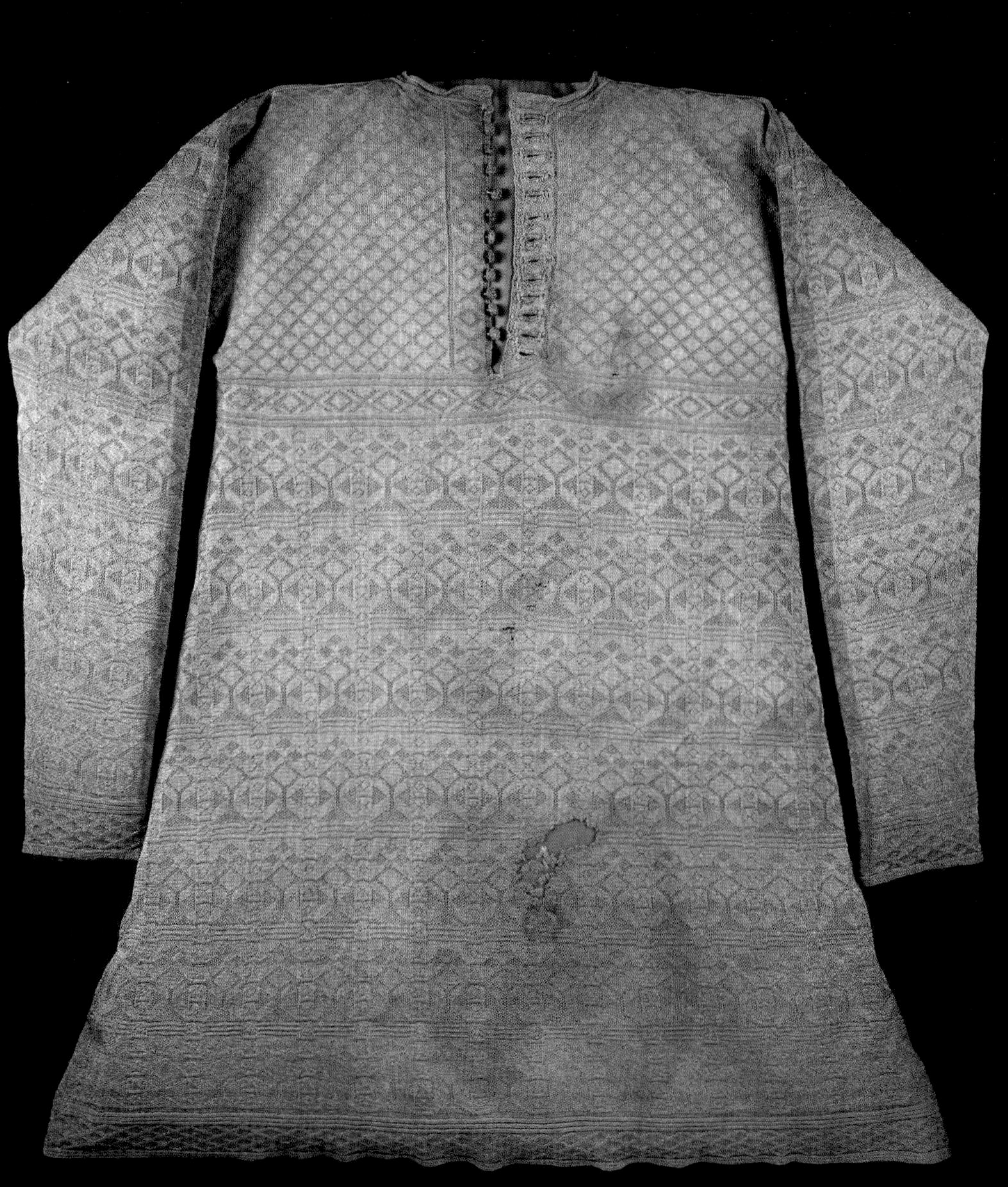

THIRTY-NINE

Charles I's shirt

This is one of the two shirts worn by King Charles I on 30 January 1649 as he stepped onto the wooden platform erected by the Banqueting House on Whitehall for his execution. He wore a second shirt to avoid shivering, not from fear but from the bitter cold. 'I am a martyr of the people,' he said, tucking his hair into his cap and poignantly asking the masked executioner 'is my hair well?' The block was deliberately reduced in size so the king had to lie flat to die, his humiliation complete. 'Stay for the sign,' were his last words, and as he gestured the axe fell, removing his head in a single blow.

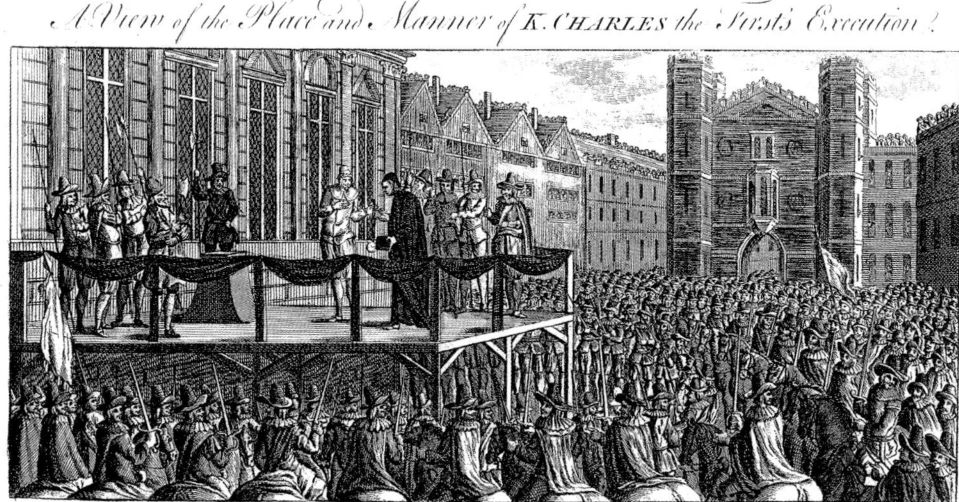

A View of the Place and Manner of K. CHARLES the First's Execution.

FORTY

King Charles I's head

In spring 1813, workmen in the crypt of St George's Chapel at Windsor Castle accidentally broke through a wall and discovered the lost vault of King Henry VIII. Inside were four coffins: the first was Henry's, the second was Jane Seymour's, the third was of a child of Queen Anne and beneath it the fourth, wrapped in black velvet, was labelled 'King Charles 1648' (Britain was yet to adopt the Gregorian Calendar). King George IV attended the exhumation. His doctor, Henry Haldane, later described the corpse: 'The cartilage of the nose was gone; but the left eye, in the first moment of exposure, was open and full, though it vanished almost immediately: and the pointed beard, so characteristic of the period … was perfect.' His left ear was also perfectly preserved, and his 'beautiful dark brown' hair, cropped short, could still be seen at the back of the head. This head was loose in the coffin. According to Clarendon's history, King Charles' body spent the night before his interment in his Windsor bedroom. As his coffin was carried to the chapel, its black velvet pall was turned white by falling snow. No burial service was read over the king's remains.

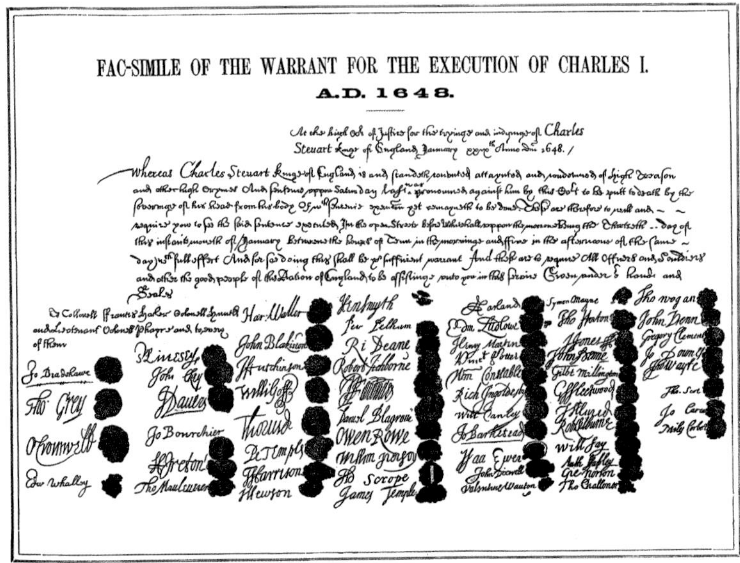

FAC-SIMILE OF THE WARRANT FOR THE EXECUTION OF CHARLES I.

A.D. 1648.

At the high Court of Justice for the tryinge and judginge of Charles Steuart Kinge of England January xxix Anno Dni 1648.

Whereas Charles Steuart Kinge of England is and standeth convicted attaynted and condemned of High Treason and other high Crymes And sentence uppon Saturday last was pronounced against him by this Court to be putt to death by the severinge of his head from his body Of wch sentence execucon yet remayneth to be done These are therefore to will and require you to see the said sentence executed In the open Streete before Whitehall uppon the morrowe being the Thirtieth day of this instante moneth of January betweene the houres of Tenn in the morninge and Five in the afternoone of the same day wth full effect And for soe doing this shall be yor sufficient warrant And these are to require All Officers and Souldiers and other the good people of this Nation of England to be assistinge unto you in this service Given under our hands and Seales

To Collonell Ffrancis Hacker Colonell Huncks and Leiutenant Colonell Phayre and to every of them

FORTY-ONE

Invitation to Charles II's autopsy

The day after King Charles II's death, 7 February 1684 (1685 by today's calendar), Dr Christian Harrell received this invitation from the Lord Chamberlain's office, requesting his presence at the king's autopsy. Harrell attended the king in his final illness, and did the same for Nell Gwynn; the Royal College of Physicians' website includes a receipt reprinted in *The Times* in 1875 which reads, 'Received by the hands of Mr Child the summe of one hondert and nine pound yn full of all remedes and medecins delivered to Mrs Ellin Gwyn deceased – I say received by me this 17th of November, 1688. Christianus Harrell.' In accordance with royal custom at the time the king's entrails were taken from his body during this autopsy and buried in separate jars.

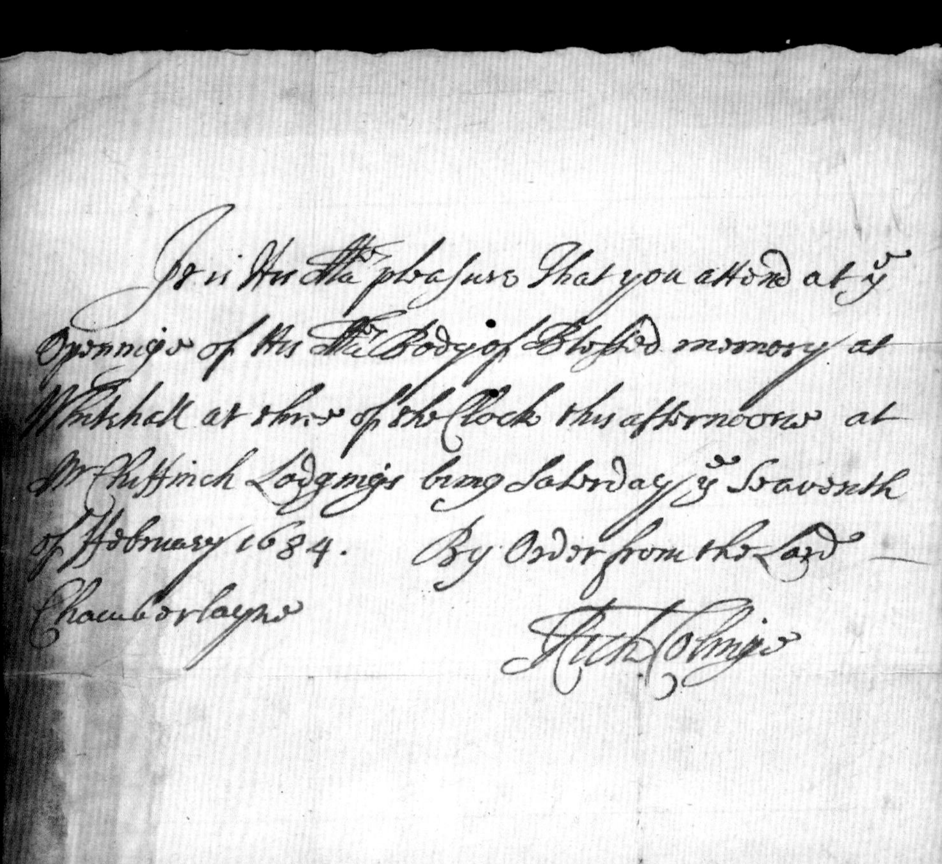

It is His Maties pleasure That you attend at ye
Openinge of the late Ks Body of Blessed memory at
Whitehall at three of the Clock this afternoone at
Mr Chiffinch Lodgings being Saterday ye Seaventh
of ffebruary 1684. By Order from the Lord
Chamberlayne

Rich Colinge

FORTY-TWO

Oliver Cromwell's coffin shield

This escutcheon, or shield bearing a coat of arms, decorated Oliver Cromwell's hearse. It featured the arms of the Commonwealth and a large crown and was one of over 2,000 escutcheons made for the occasion, at a cost of £600. The lion rampant on the left is Cromwell's family symbol; the leopards on the right are his wife's. This particular 'taffety' (silk) flag cost ten shillings to make. Only four now survive. The most exciting is kept at Westminster School: a seventeenth-century pupil called Robert Uvedale snatched it during the funeral, framed it and wrote an account of his theft on the back. In 2015 it appeared on the *Antiques Roadshow*, where it was valued at £25,000.

FORTY-THREE

Lady Fanshawe's plague cure recipe

The plague returned with a vengeance in the seventeenth century and every means was employed to avoid it. This recipe is from the collection of Anne, Lady Fanshawe, who was married to Charles I's secretary of war, had fourteen children, travelled through Europe and attended on the exiled Charles II. The concoction of malmsey, sage and pepper here would perhaps have been more cheering than efficacious, but the author is confident: 'In all your plague time under God trust to this: for there was never none died of the Plague that tooke it.' This wax plague scene from the Science Museum, made in 1657, attempts to capture the horrors seen during times of plague. The tomb inscription reads, pointedly, 'My lot today, yours tomorrow.'

r;

Dr. Burges his Directions in tyme of Plague.

three pints of Malmsey, boile in it a handfull of Sage a
ll of Rue, till a pinte be wasted, then straine it and sett
ye fire againe, and putt thereto a penny worth of long Pepper
an ounce of Ginger, a Quarter of an Ounce of Nutmegs, all
together. then let it boile a little, and take it of the Fire, &
it 4 pennyworth of Mithridate, 2 pennyworth of treacle
arter of a pint of the best Angelico water. keepe this as your
bove all wordly treasure. take it alwaies warme both morning
ening a Spoonfull or two if You be infected, and sweat thereupon
You be not infected then one spoonefull a day is sufficient, half
full in the morning and halfe at night. In all Your Plague
nder God trust to this. for there was never none died of the
that tooke it. This is not only good for the Common Plague
r the Measells, Small Poxe, Surfetts, and divers other kind
ases.

To make Lozenges for a Cold.

FORTY-FOUR

Jonathan Swift's margin notes

These crisp annotations in the margins of *Memoirs of the secret services of John Macky, esq., during the reigns of King William, Queen Anne, and King George I,* mini-biographies of notable men assembled by the Scottish spy John Macky, were made by the acerbic Jonathan Swift, author of *Gulliver's Travels* and Dean of St Patrick's Cathedral in Dublin. His notes were carefully copied into a few extant volumes by friends and acquaintances. Each is a masterpiece of caustic brevity, most notably the word 'no' next to the word 'virtue' in the Earl of Sunderland's entry. His insults are withering: the Duke of Grafton was 'almost a slobberer, without any good quality', the Earl of Sandwich 'very ugly and a fop' and the Archbishop of Canterbury 'the most good for nothing prelate I ever knew'. Charles, Duke of Bolton, 'does not now make any figure at Court', the guide notes; 'Nor anywhere else – a great Booby,' added Swift. He died in 1745 and his own epitaph for his memorial in St Patrick's churchyard says that he lies 'where savage indignation can no longer tear his heart.'

56 CHARACTERS *of the*

in the Reign of this Queen He is ſtill one of the pleaſanteſt Companions in the World, when he likes his Company. He is very fat, troubled with the Spleen, and turned of ſixty Years old.

not of late years but a Very dull one.

John, Lord *Somers*, late Lord Chancellor,

Very mean His father was a noted rogue.

OF a creditable Family, in the City of *Worceſter*; his Father was an Attorney, and bred him to the Law, which was his Profeſſion for ſome Years, before he was taken notice of. He was retained as one of the Counſel for the ſeven Biſhops in King *James*'s Reign; and behaved himſelf, in that Cauſe, with ſo much Applauſe, as gained him a very great Reputation, and firſt brought him into Buſineſs.

On King *William*'s Acceſſion to the Throne, he was made Attorney General, Lord Keeper, Lord Chancellor, and a Peer; and was for many Years Chief in the Adminiſtration of publick Affairs.

FORTY-FIVE

Sir Christopher Wren's report

Sir Christopher Wren, busy rebuilding St Paul's Cathedral after the Great Fire of London, had been wrangling with the City authorities for years when he sent this report to the Lands Committee in 1675. In it he listed options for the top of the planned Monument to the Great Fire. He had considered a phoenix ('dangerous by reason of the sayle the spread winges will carry in the winde') or a 12-foot statue, but approved the king's choice of a large gilt ball with flames for decoration 'by reson of the good appeareance at distance and because one may goe up into it, and upon occasion use it for fireworkes'. The 'belcony', he insisted, 'must be made of substantiall well forged worke', for which the bill should not exceed 'fowrscore and ten poundes'. The Monument still stands today.

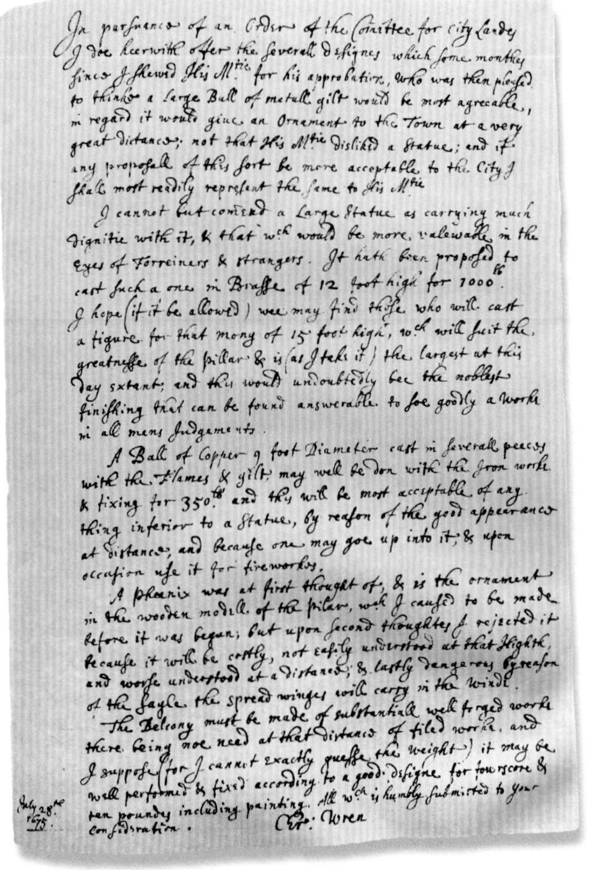

FORTY-SIX

Charles II's coronation medal

This medal commemorates an extraordinary moment in British history: the restoration of a king. Charles II is pictured in his coronation robes with the Order of the Garter's medal around his neck. His father Charles I was wearing this Order – his 'George', with the motto *Honi soit qui mal y pense* ('evil to him who evil thinks') picked out in tiny diamonds – at his execution. It was sold afterwards and had to be recovered for his son with a lawsuit. The likeness of the thirty-year old king on this medal was said to be a good one and the reverse shows him on the throne, being crowned by an angel, with the motto *everso missus succurrere seculo* ('Sent to restore a fallen age') and the date, 23 April 1661.

FORTY-SEVEN

John Milton's publishing contract

This elegant document is the contract between John Milton, gentleman, and Samuel Symons, printer, signed by the poet when already blind (as he was when he dictated the whole of *Paradise Lost*). The signature was done for him and his personal seal added, impressed with his own hands. It gave Symons and his executors the 'full benefitt, proffitt and advantage' of sales of *Paradise Lost*, in return for 'the summ of five pounds of lawfull English money', plus £5 for each of the next three editions – quite a bargain for one of the most famous works in all of English literature.

FORTY-EIGHT

King James I's book

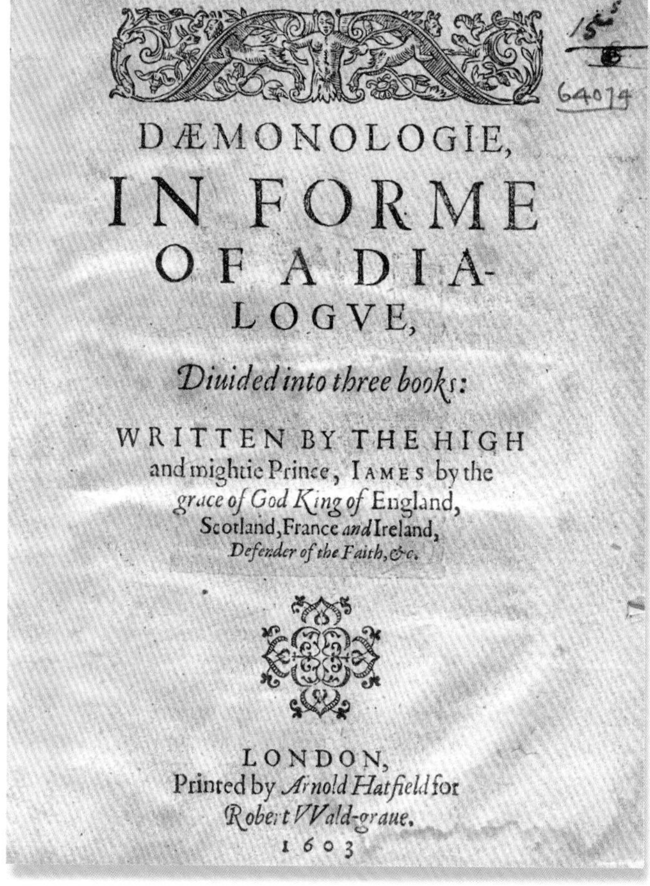

DÆMONOLOGIE,
IN FORME
OF A DIA-
LOGVE,
Diuided into three books:
WRITTEN BY THE HIGH
and mightie Prince, IAMES by the
grace of God King of England,
Scotland, France *and* Ireland,
Defender of the Faith, &c.

LONDON,
Printed by *Arnold Hatfield* for
Robert VValdgraue.
1603

James, 'by the grace of God King of England, Scotland, France and Ireland', was also an author. *Daemonologie, In Forme of a Dialogue, Divided into three books, by James Rx* was actually written in 1597 as part of his fight against 'the fearefull aboundinge at this time in this countrie, of these detestable slaves of the Devil, the Witches or enchaunters'. His Witchcraft Act of 1604 was used against the witches in Salem, Massachusetts, and he fervently believed that witches had once tried to drown him as he crossed the Channel, a theory confirmed by the terrified old women caught, tortured and personally questioned by him on reaching Scotland. A rival volume, *The Discoverie of Witchcraft,* attempted to explode the notion of the existence of witches: when he took the English throne in 1603, James ordered all copies burned.

FORTY-NINE

The Duke of Monmouth's plea

The 1st Duke of Monmouth, illegitimate son of the late King Charles II, was in trouble. His rebellion against King James II had failed and he needed allies. This letter, sent to Charles' Dowager Queen Catherine, the new king's sister-in-law, was a desperate plea for help. 'Being in this unfortunate condition, and having non left but your Majesty that I think may have some compassion for me … makes me take this boldnes to beg of you to intersed for me,' he wrote. 'I hope, Madam, your intersision will give me life to repent of it, and to shew the king how realy and truly I will serve him hear after'. It didn't: the Duke's beheading, horribly botched by the executioner, took place on Tower Hill on 15 July 1685.

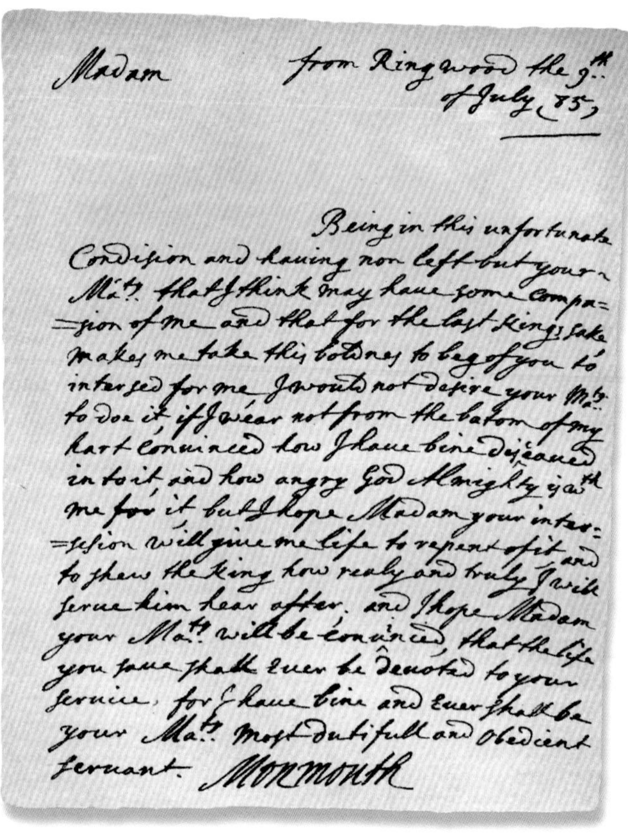

Madam   from Ringwood the 9th of July (85)

Being in this unfortunate Condision and having non left but your Maty that I think may have some compa=sion of me and that for the last Kings sake makes me take this boldnes to beg of you to interseed for me I would not desire your Maty to doe it if I wear not from the botom of my hart convinced how I have bine deceaved into it and how angry God Almighty is with me for it but I hope Madam your inter=sesion will give me life to repent of it and to shew the King how realy and truly I will serve him hear after. and I hope Madam your Maty will be convinced, that the life you save shall ever be devoted to your service, for I have bine and ever shall be your Maty most dutifull and Obedient servant. Monmouth

FIFTY

William III's instructions

These dramatic orders from William III to Admiral Herbert, later Earl of Torrington, were dispatched from the court at Whitehall on 16 March 1689, written by the Earl of Nottingham but signed and initialled by the king. Dutch William and his English wife Mary, daughter of the deposed James II, took their joint thrones after the Glorious Revolution. James fled to the Continent, dropping the Great Seal into the Thames *en route*. Here the admiral is instructed to deliver the captured king into the approved 'persons hands'. But, the new king cautions, 'In case you shall take any ship or vessell in which the late King James shall happen to be, you are to treat him with respect.'

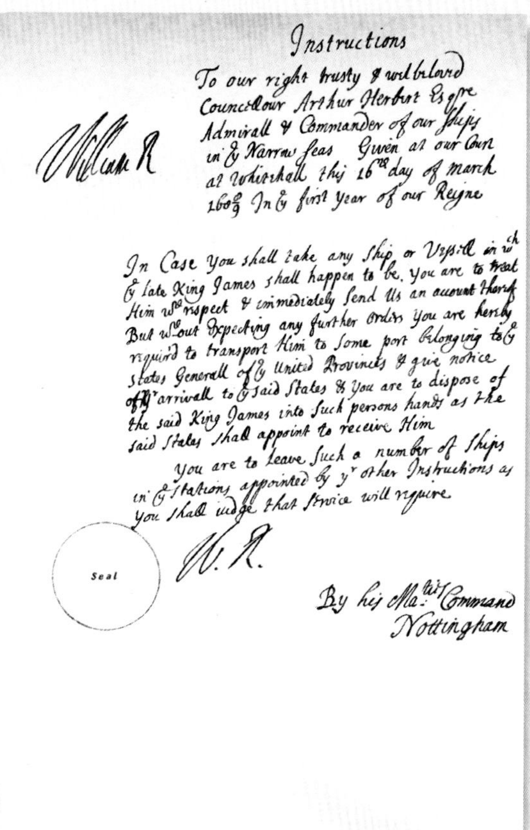

Instructions

William R

To our right trusty & welbeloved Councellour Arthur Herbert Esqre Admirall & Commander of our Ships in ye Narrow seas Given at our Court at Whitehall this 16th day of March 1688/9 In ye first year of our Reigne

In Case you shall take any Ship or Vessell in wch ye late King James shall happen to be, You are to treat Him wth respect & immediately send Us an account thereof But wthout Expecting any further Orders You are hereby required to transport Him to Some port belonging to ye States Generall of ye United Provinces & give notice of his arrivall to ye said States & You are to dispose of the said King James into Such persons hands as the said States shall appoint to receive Him

You are to leave Such a number of Ships in ye Stations appointed by yr other Instructions as You shall iudge that Service will require

W. R.

Seal

By his Maties Command
Nottingham

FIFTY-ONE

Lord Lovat's execution block

This execution block, still on display at the Tower of London, was used for Simon Fraser, 11th Lord Lovat and the last man in Britain to be executed by beheading. Lovat joined 'the '45' (Jacobite Rebellion of 1745) and was accused of High Treason. He conducted his own defence – described by Horace Walpole, Earl of Orford, as 'villainy, wound up by buffoonery' – and was sentenced to hanging, drawing and quartering. This was commuted to beheading, for which he practised kneeling using a cushion. On Tower Hill he was notably insouciant, testing the axe blade, paying the executioner for a clean blow, examining his own coffin plate (pictured) and muttering *Dulce et decorum est pro Patria moro* ('tis a glorious end to die for one's country) before dropping his handkerchief as a signal for the axe to fall. The coffin plates were found during the building of Victorian barracks at the Tower.

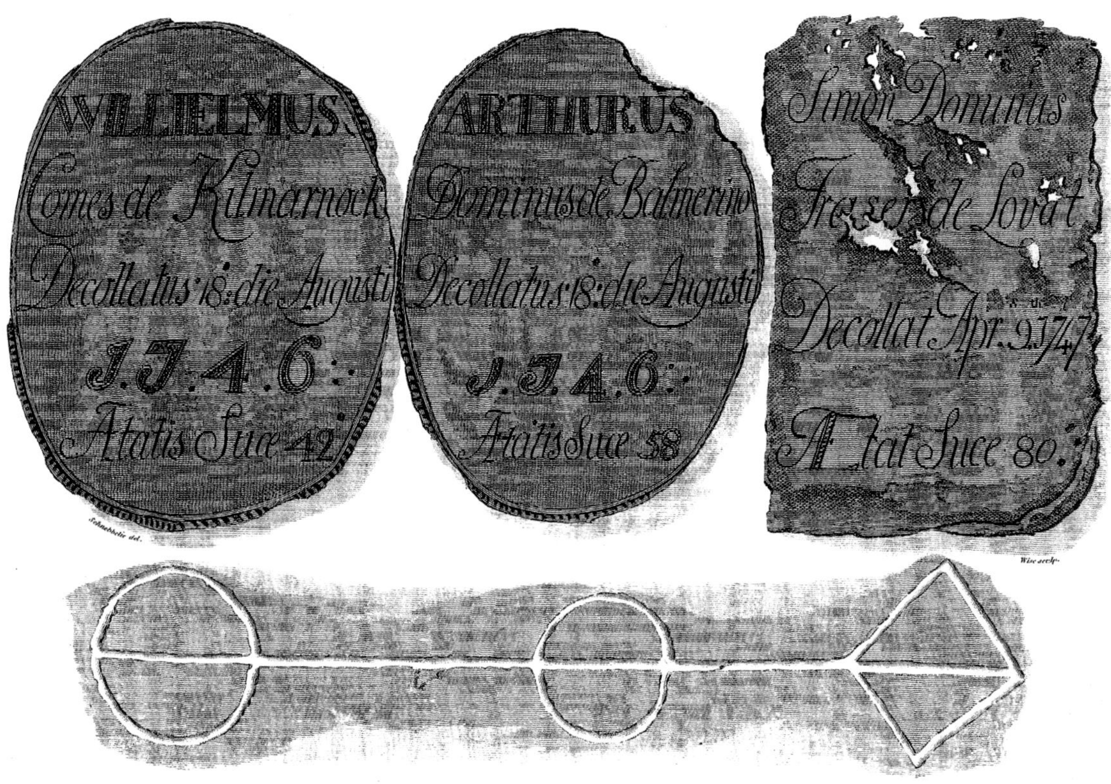

THE COFFIN PLATES OF THE REBEL LORDS, WHO WERE EXECUTED ON TOWER HILL 1746 & 1747.

London Published Oct.r 11th 1816 by R. Wilkinson. No. 125 Fenchurch Str.

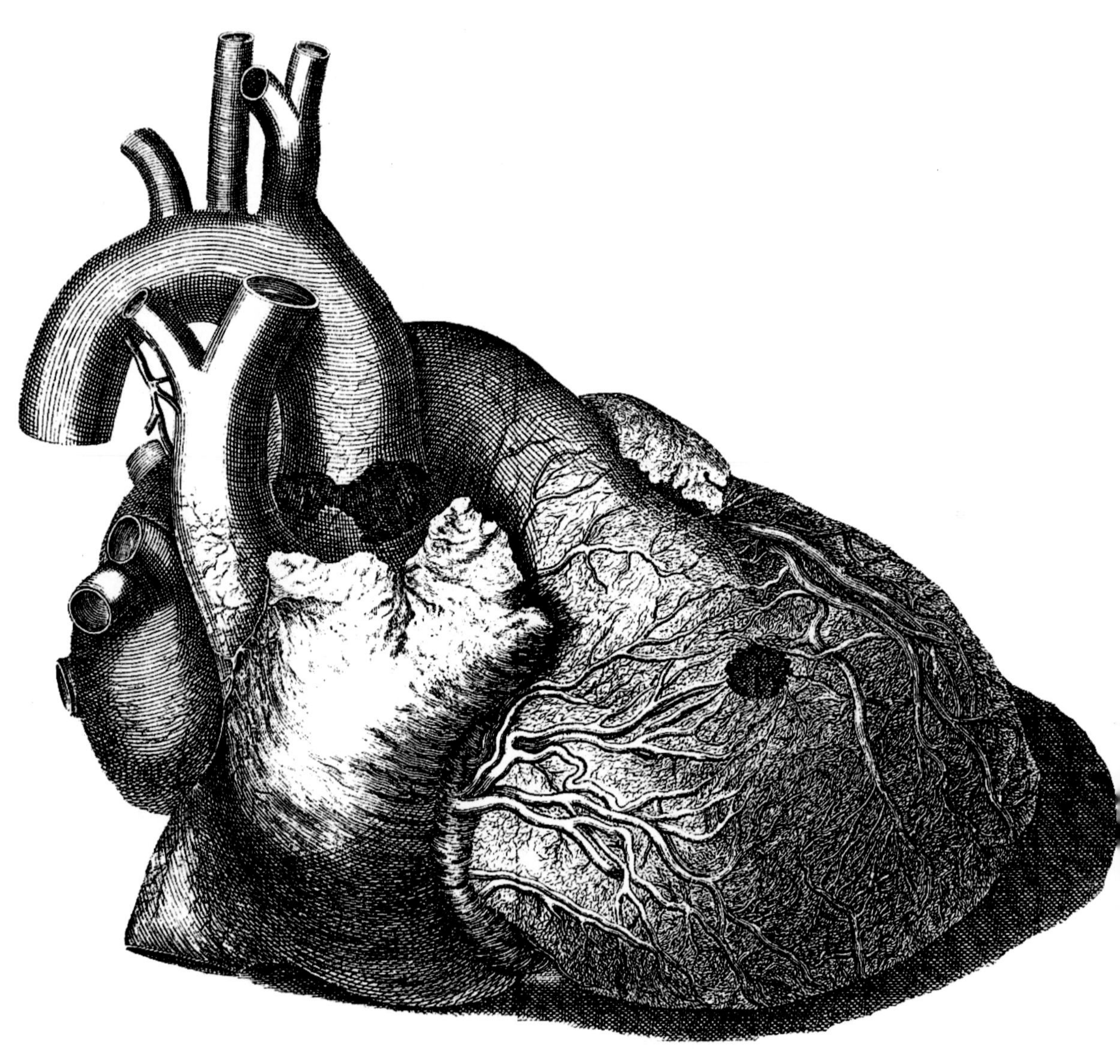

FIFTY-TWO

George II's heart

This engraving shows the ruptured heart of the second Hanoverian king. It finally gave up on him as he sat on the lavatory on 25 October 1760. There was, it was said, a crash heard throughout Kensington Palace, 'as if a large billet was tumbling down'. The autopsy report sent to the President of the Royal Society described 'a quantity of coagulated blood, nearly sufficient to fill a pint cup'. Beneath it was this hole, 'large enough to admit the extremity of the little finger ... his Majesty must, therefore, have dropped down, and died instantaneously'. The doctor thought the cause must have been 'pressure on all the contents of the lower belly...' from 'his Majesty having been at the necessary-stool'. Indeed the king had 'complained of frequent distresses and sinkings about the region of the heart' for some years beforehand. The heart and its vessels were filled with wax to take this sketch.

FIFTY-THREE

George III's hair

King George III, 'Squire George', was the first of his dynasty to be born in Britain, a fact he was keen to point out in the first speech he made after his accession to the throne. This paragraph, in his own hand, was a late addition. 'Born and educated in this country,' he wrote, 'I glory in the name of Britain; and the peculiar happiness of my life will ever consist in promoting the welfare of a people whose loyalty and warm affection I consider as the greatest and most permanent security of my Throne.' The collector Henry Wellcome bought this lock of the king's hair in the 1920s: when tested, it was found to contain high levels of arsenic, aggravating the medical condition, probably porphyria, now thought to have caused his insanity.

\+ Born & Educated in this Country I glory in the Name of Britain, & the peculiar happiness of my Life, will ever consist in promoting the Welfare of a people, whose Loyalty & warm affection to me, I consider, as the greatest & most permanent Security of my Throne.

FIFTY-FOUR

Keats' last hope

The poet John Keats trained as a surgeon-apothecary at Guy's Hospital and although he never practised he knew enough to know that he was ill. 'I am excessively nervous,' he wrote to his sister Fanny from Wentworth Place, the house he shared with Fanny Brawne's family in Hampstead, adding 'tis not yet Consumption I believe, but it would be were I to remain in this climate all the winter; so I am thinking of either voyageing or travelling to Italy. Yesterday I received an invitation from Mr Shelley [the poet], a gentleman residing at Pisa, to spend the winter with him.' In vain did he hope that time and health would produce some more poems for Fanny to read: he never reached Pisa, but died in Rome on 23 February 1821. All his published poetry was completed in just six years.

staying a short time with Mr Brawne who lives in the House which was Mr Dilke's. I am excessively nervous: a person I am not quite used to entering the room half chokes me. 'Tis not yet Consumption I believe, but it would be were I to remain in this climate all the Winter: so I am thinking of either voyaging or travelling to Italy. Yesterday I received an invitation from Mr Shelley, a Gentleman residing at Pisa, to spend the Winter with him: if I go I must be away in a Month or even less. I am glad you like the Poems you must hope with me th[at] time and health will pro[duce] you some more. This is the first morning I have been able to sit to the paper and have many Letters to write if I can manage them. God bless you my dear Sister.

Your affectionate Brother

John -

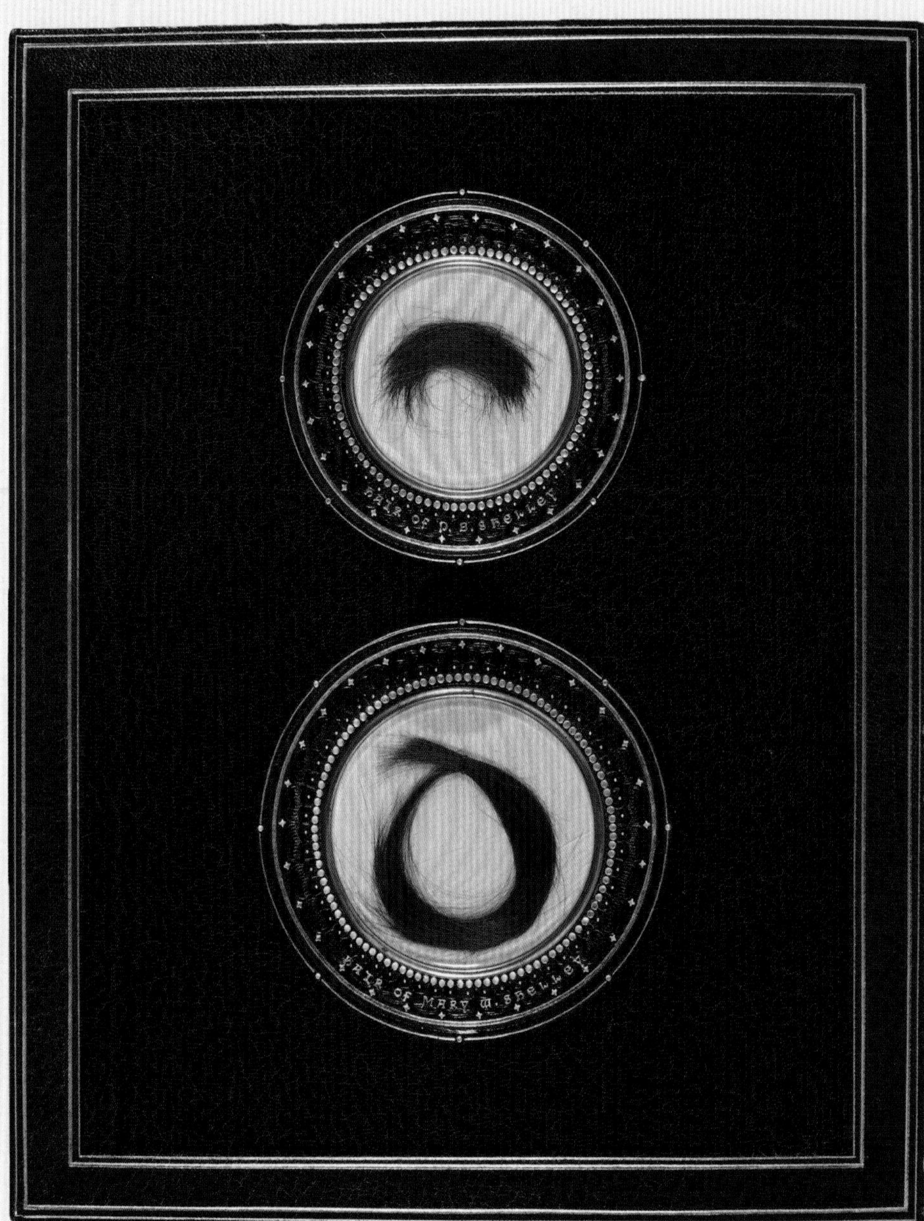
HAIR OF P. B. SHELLEY
HAIR OF MARY W. SHELLEY

FIFTY-FIVE

Percy Bysshe Shelley's hair

Percy Bysshe Shelley, who kept his hair long and hanging over his eyes, drowned in Italy just before his thirtieth birthday. When his body washed ashore it was buried on the beach. A month later a friend, Edward John Trelawny, had the poet exhumed and cremated in order to bring him home. Trelawny found himself 'paralysed with the sharp and thrilling noise a spade made in coming in direct contact with the skull'. He recorded the whole gruesome process with almost indecent relish, describing the poet's face stripped by fish, his skull stained indigo with the lime thrown onto the corpse, and watching as 'the brains literally seethed, bubbled, and boiled as in a cauldron' on his funeral pyre. The heart, snatched from the fire, was kept by Shelley's wife, some said in an ornamental urn on the mantlepiece and others in a desk drawer, wrapped in a page torn from one of his books. It was finally buried in 1889, with the body of Shelley's son Sir Percy. Trelawny, having refused to let Lord Byron keep the skull, as 'he had formerly used one as a drinking cup', went on to make a healthy living writing about his friendships with the Romantic poets.

FIFTY-SIX

Bedlam's boxes

Bethlem Hospital was founded in London in 1247 but the first mention of mental illness was two centuries later. Over the years, thanks to corrupt administrators, fraudulent doctors and punitive attitudes, its name – shortened to Bedlam – became synonymous with chaos and horror. These alms boxes stood outside the Moorfields building, infamous for its public openings with chained and raving inmates on show like animals in a zoo. In 1815 the hospital moved to St George's Fields in South London and this architect's plan shows more progressive thinking: men and women were properly separated, with the criminally insane in a detached block; it was light and airy and even had warm baths. The hospital moved out to Bromley in the 1930s; the building now houses the Imperial War Museum.

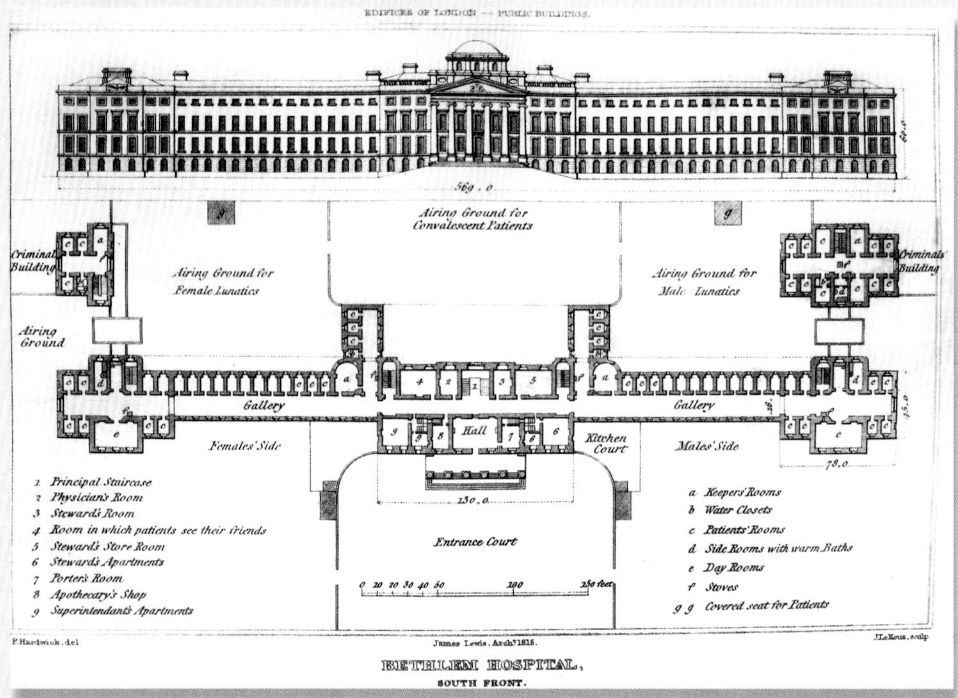

FIFTY-SEVEN

Edward Jenner's lancets

It seems scarcely credible to the modern mind that the physician Edward Jenner tested his theory of vaccination in 1796 by deliberately infecting the eight-year old son of his gardener with cowpox, a milder version of the virulent, disfiguring disease smallpox. We are lucky he did. The Jenner Museum estimates that smallpox killed up to 10 per cent of the population and while vaccination existed – Jenner himself was vaccinated at school – his cowpox vaccine was far safer. He used these ivory points, coated in pus from a cowpox blister, to scratch the skin of a healthy patient. The steel lancets, in their handsome tortoiseshell case, were used for bloodletting as well as vaccination. This lock of hair was cut after Jenner's death.

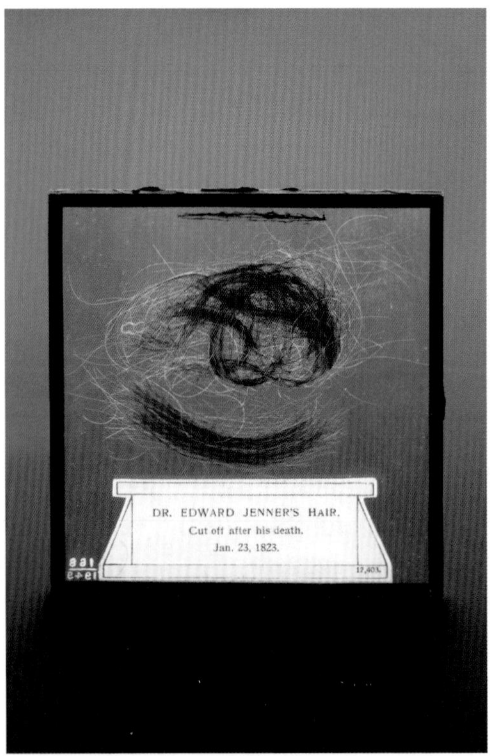

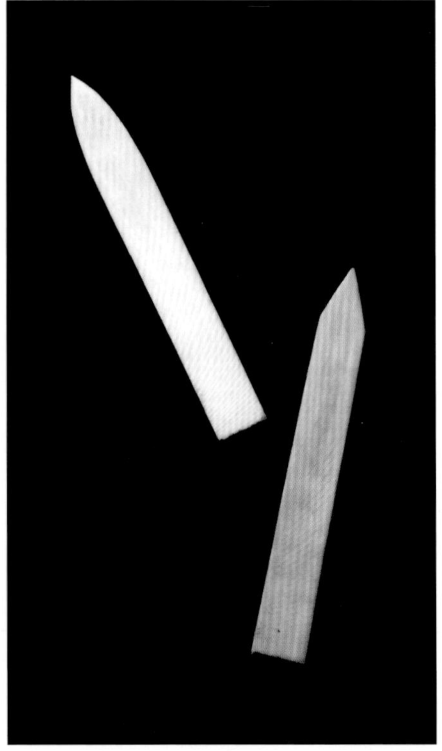

WEISS
LONDON
WEISS
LONDON

FIFTY-EIGHT

Jeremy Bentham's skin

The philosopher Jeremy Bentham could never be accused of hypocrisy. A firm rationalist, after his death in 1832 and according to his instructions he was publicly dissected and displayed; what he called his 'auto-icon' (his skeleton, wearing his clothes, stuffed with hay, and topped with a wax head sporting his own hair) still sits in a box in University College London. His mummified head was displayed too, but became a target for pranks so is now stored. This strip of skin comes from the dissection. The inscription reads: 'Part of the skin of the late Jeremy Bentham Esq. who bequeathed his Body for anatomical purposes, and was dissected, July 1832.' In an interesting aside, Bentham was dissected in one of the very theatres supplied by the man in the next item.

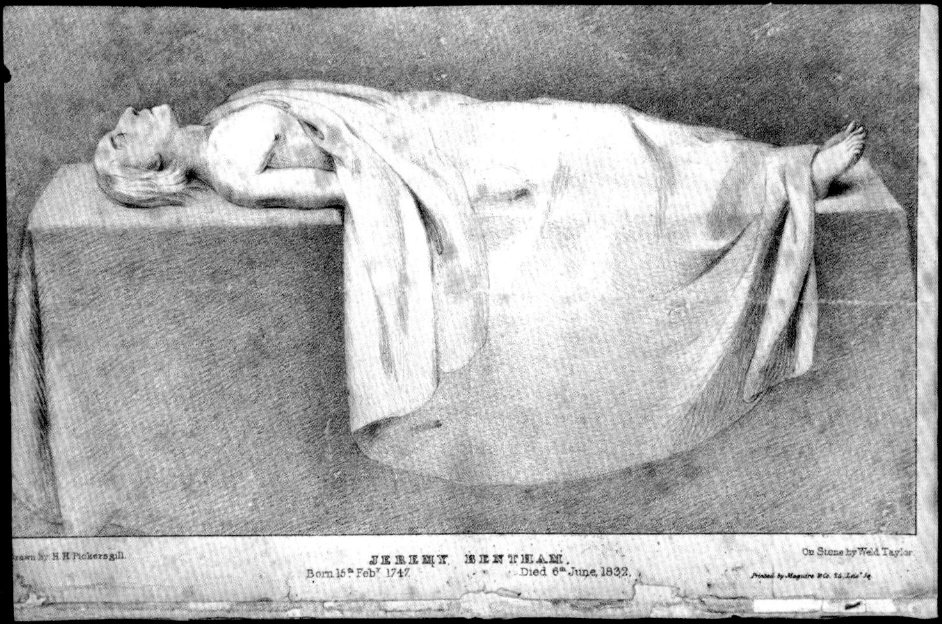

rawn by H H Pickersgill.

JEREMY BENTHAM.

Born 15th Feby 1747. Died 6th June, 1832.

On Stone by Weld Taylor

FIFTY-NINE

A bodysnatcher's poem

Here is the last poem of a condemned man who did not die. This poem was penned by the bodysnatcher James May, condemned to die at the age of thirty for selling a murder victim to the surgeons at University College. May was in a gang exploiting the growing demand for corpses by doping homeless youths with opium and drowning them. May specialised in removing teeth, worth as much as a colossal £2 a set when repurposed as dentures. When the surgeons called the police, May was so drunk he had to crawl into the interrogation room, claiming he thought that the body had been stolen, and had not known the subject had been murdered. At the very last minute – his hanging chains were up – his death sentence was commuted. He fainted 'as if struck by lightning' and then, still shaking, shook hands with the prison guards and with his former friends. The two other gang members were then hanged and dissected – at King's College and at Windmill Street, two of the places they had previously supplied with bodies to dissect.

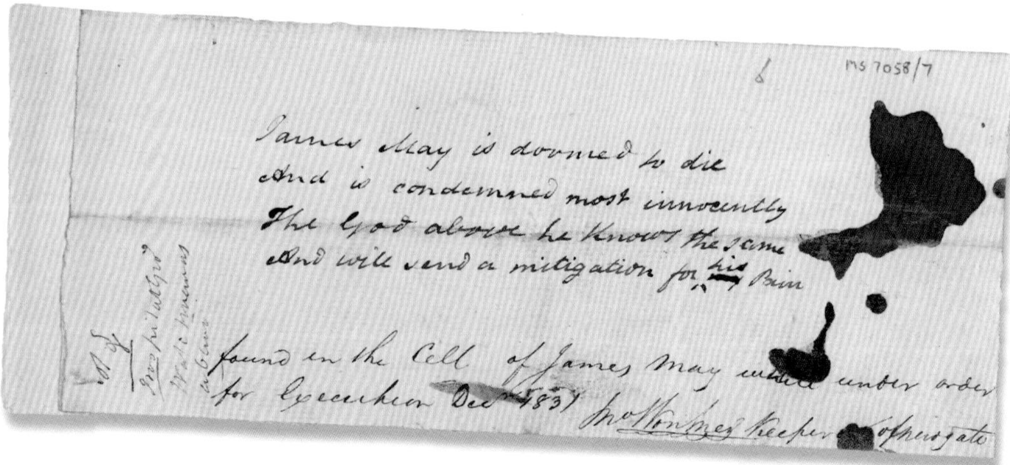

Ms 7058/7

James May is doomed to die
And is condemned most innocently
The God above he knows the same
And will send a mitigation for his Pain

found in the Cell of James May while under order
for Execution Dec 1831
Mr Wontner Keeper of Newgate

(1831)

On Thursday the 3rd day of November, I Thomas Williams saw a Boy asleep in the Pig Market Smithfield I gave him a penny and he Bought a penny worth of Pudding. I then took him to the Bell Public House at the Top of the Pig Market and gave him a Half pint of Beer for which I paid about half an hour afterwards I fetched him out the Pot Boy or Landladys Son followed me out with another Drover opposite the Door I told the Boy to watch up the Court and see that no one came out with a Bed. I then went to the Fortune of War Public House and waited there about ½ an Hour I then went and fetched him and took him to the Old Bailey Watering House and left him outside and told him to wait there I then went to the ~~Water~~ Fortune of War to see if Bishop Was there and he was not – I then went back to the Boy and there met Bishop We went ~~up~~ Ludgate Hill thro Cheapside Home me Bishop and the Boy We had a pint of Stout in Aldersgate Street We had nothing else till we got Home Bishop went and got some Rum and I gave him very Nigh a Quartern with a Portion of Laudanum in it the Boy laid down and went to sleep on the Floor ~~when~~ asleep Bishop took the Boy up in his Arms and put him Head first into the Water Butt which is sunk in the ground and I assisted him he there died and me and Bishop Stripped him and put him in the Box where he remained until May saw him on Friday Night. Before We Brought him home And ~~afterwards~~ We asked ~~him~~ What his Name was and where he came from he told us his Name was White that he had no relation but one Brother and to the best of my recollection he said his brother was a Sailor abroad and came from Lincolnshire I asked him how he came to London and to the best of my recollection he said he came up with a Country Drover from Lincolnshire with some Sheep and

SIXTY

Byron's legal letter

There is defiance in this letter from Lord Byron to his solicitor John Hanson, who has suggested selling the family estate, Newstead Abbey, to pay off his debts. Byron, then living in some penury in Greece, inherited Newstead – and possibly some of his characteristics – from his great-uncle William, 'the Wicked Lord'. The latter once threw a human corpse into his wife's coach and ruined the Newstead estate – felling trees, slaughtering deer – to punish his son, who refused to marry as instructed. The son died, and Byron got the estate instead. 'it is in the power of God, the Devil, and man, to make me poor and miserable,' he wrote grimly, 'but neither the second or the third shall make me sell Newstead'. He was finally forced to comply in 1817.

Athens. Nov:

Dear Sir,

Yours arrived on
it tells me I am ruined. —
power of God, the Devil, and
me poor and miserable, but n
nor third shall make me sell
by the aid of the first I will
this resolution. — — My fa
not be made a den of thieves.
shall not be sold. — — I
miles from home with few resou
prospect of their daily becoming
neither friend nor counsellor,
servant departs with this letter
is forlorn enough for a man of
former expectations, — do not n
complaint however, I state the
will never degrade myself
You have my answer. — —
Commend me to your fa

t 1810.

first Inst.
- is in the
r, to make
the second
ewstead, and
rsevere in
's house shall
Newstead
some thousand
and the
s, I have
only English
my situation
my birth and
ke this for
mple fact, and
lamentations.

y, I perceive

Hargreaves is your partner, he always
promised to turn out well, and Charles
I am sure is a very fine fellow. – As
for the others I can't pretend to pro=
=phecy. I present my respects to all the
ladies, and I suppose I may kiss Harriet
as you or Mrs. Hanson will be my proxy,
provided she is not grown too tall for
such a token of remembrance. –
I must not forget Mrs Hanson who has
often been a mother to me, and as you have
always been a friend I beg you to believe me
with all sincerity

yours Byron

J. Hanson Esqre.
6. Chancery Lane
London

SIXTY-ONE

Georgian *memento mori*

The inevitability of death has been with us since time began, and the *memento mori* ('remember that you must die') is an object designed to remind us of the fact. Even the confident Romans handed out *larva convivialis* like this model skeleton to their guests; Mary, Queen of Scots famously had a skull-shaped watch, while the tombs in our churches often boast hour-glasses or scythes. This oddly charming dead-and-alive pair are beautifully crafted Georgian examples from the Wellcome Collection. The life expectancy then was still only around forty; Jane Austen, one of our most beloved Georgian figures, died at the age of just forty-one. However, the wealthy, as ever, could usually expect to live longer, and reaching the sixth or seventh decade would not have been viewed as unusual in this era.

SIXTY-TWO

Nelson's Spyglass

When Admiral Lord Nelson was felled by a sniper at the moment of his greatest triumph at Trafalgar, it was far from his first brush with death. He lost the sight in one eye at Calvi (1794) and his right arm at Santa Cruz (1797), when, in a fine example of British *sang froid*, he returned to his flagship, had the arm – which was shattered by a musket ball – removed and continued giving orders. Nelson wrote that night's report with his left hand. This screw was used during the surgery to loosen or tighten the tourniquet's fabric. The surgery was performed during the night and at sea, and the result caused Nelson great pain. A nerve at the end of his arm was caught in the silk ligatures (the thread around the blood vessel), producing 'a constant irritation and discharge'. Every day, a surgeon would come by and pull on the threads to see if they were ready to come free, causing agony. They remained, and he in pain, for three months before it finally came loose. In the meantime, Nelson's wife dressed his wound herself. When he met the king soon afterwards, Nelson famously declared, 'so long as I have a foot to stand on, I will combat for my king and country.' Compensation for his lost eye, meanwhile, was initially refused, as he had no doctor's certificate. When he returned with the paperwork the clerk expressed surprise at the small amount due. 'Oh! This is only for an eye,' said Nelson breezily, 'In a few days I shall come for an arm; and in a little time longer, God knows, most probably for a leg.'

SIXTY-THREE

Nelson's last letter

Two days before Trafalgar, Nelson wrote this letter to his mistress Emma, Lady Hamilton, who started her career dancing naked on the tables at an aristocratic house party aged fifteen and eventually married the noted antiquarian Sir William Hamilton. Nelson was writing in the Captain's cabin of the *Victory* on 19 October 1805. 'My Dearest beloved Emma,' he began, ending, 'I hope in God that I shall live to finish my letter after the battle.' Instead Captain Hardy brought her this letter, 'found open on His Desk'; he never had the chance to use the seal he used when writing to Emma (an example of which is given here). The postscript, in Emma's hand, reads, 'Oh miserable wretched Emma. Oh glorious and happy Nelson.' She died ten years later in Calais.

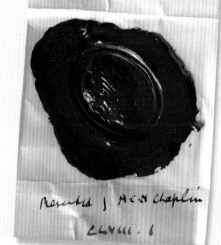

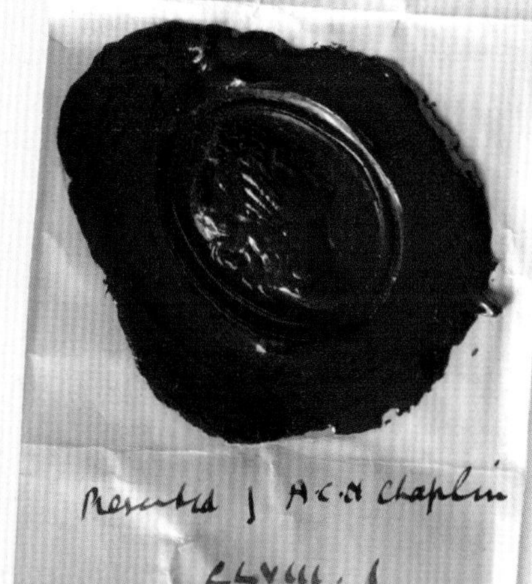

Battle, may heaven bless you prays your Nelson & Bronte. Oct[r]. 20th in the morning we were close to the mouth of the Streights but the Wind had not come far enough to the Westward to allow the Combined Fleets to Weather the Shoals off Trafalgar but they were counted as far as forty Sail of Ships of War which I suppose to be 34 of the Line and Six frigates, a Group of them was seen off the Lighthouse of Cadiz this Morn[g] but it blows so very fresh & thick weather that I rather believe they will go into the Harbour before Night, May God almighty give us success over these fellows and enable us to get a Peace

This letter was found open on His Desk & brought to Lady Hamilton by Cap[n] Hardy

Oh miserable wretched Emma
Oh glorious & happy Nelson

Report of Nelson's Death

A nation desperate for every detail of Nelson's death had to depend on reports such as this, written on 15 December 1805 by Sir William Beatty, the *Victory*'s surgeon. He described the awful wounds, caused by a French sniper's ball, that would kill the admiral two hours later. Nelson, he wrote, complained of 'acute pain' and could feel a 'gush of blood every minute within his breast', telling the surgeon that his back was 'shot through'. As his limbs grew cold, he 'retained his wonted energy of mind, and exercise of his faculties, until the latest moment of his existence'. Nelson gave his last orders and perished without a struggle. Beatty later extracted the ball, still 'firmly attached' to scraps of gold lace and padding from Nelson's epaulette and coat. The blood-stained coat is in the Royal Museums Greenwich, and the ball itself is at Windsor Castle.

H: M: Ship Victor

"About the middle of the Action with the Combi
October last, the late Illustrious Commander in Chie
mortally wounded in the left breast by a Musquet
fired from the Mizen top of La Redoutable French
which the Victory fell on board of early in the batt
was in the Act of turning on the Quarter Deck w
towards the enemy, when he received his wound, h
was carried to the Cockpit where he lived about two
* "On his Lordship's being brought below, he complained
about the sixth or seventh Dorsal Vertebra, of pri
motion of the body and inferior extremities; his Re
difficult. his Pulse weak small and irregular. he freque
back was shot through; that he felt every instant a g
his breast; and that he had sensations which indica
approach of death: in the course of an hour his Pulse
and was gradually lost in the Arm, his extremities
soon afterwards cold: he retained his wonted energy
of his faculties, until the latest moment of his existen
as signal as decisive was announced to him he expre
acknowledgements thereof and heartfelt satisfaction a
event in the most emphatic language; he then deliv
with his usual precision, and in a few Minutes after ex

Course and Site of the Ball ascertained since D
The Ball struck the forepart of his Lordships Epaulette
left shoulder immediately before the Processus Acromion
slightly fractured, it then descended obliquely into the

[torn] 2 & 3d Ribs; and after penetrating the left lobe of the Lungs and dividing in its passage, a large branch of the Pulmonary Artery it entered the left side of the Spine between the sixth and seventh Dorsal Vertebræ fractured the left transverse Process of the sixth Vertebræ, wounded the Medulla Spinalis, and fracturing the right transverse Process of the seventh Vertebræ, it made its way from the right side of the Spine, directing its course through the Muscles of the back, and lodged therein, about two inches below the inferior angle of the right Scapula. —

"On removing the ball a portion of the Gold lace and Pad of the Epaulette together with a small piece of his Lordships coat were found firmly attached to it." —

W. Beatty
Surgeon

...th December
Fleets on the 21st
Lord Nelson, was
, supposed to be
...ip of the line,
his Lordship
his face &
...stantly fell, and
...ours. —
...ute pain &
...w of sense and
...ation was short &
declared his
...f blood within
to him the
...ame indistinct
forehead became
mind, and exercise
and when Victory
his pious
the Glorious
his last words
without a struggle
...th.) To
...nd entered the
...ula which it
...ræ, fracturing
the

SIXTY-FIVE

Nelson's coffin

On the bottom of this elegantly decorated coffin was a note saying: 'I do hereby certify, that every part of this coffin is made from wood and iron of 'L'Orient' most of which was picked up by His Majesty's ship under my command, in the Bay of Aboukir.' It was written by Nelson's friend Captain Hallowell, who had the coffin made from the mainmast of a French flagship Nelson blew up spectacularly at the Battle of the Nile. With it, he sent a letter: 'Herewith I send you a coffin,' it read, 'that, when you are tired of this life, you may be buried in one of your own trophies: but may that period be far distant, is the sincere wish of your obedient and much obliged servant, BEN HALLOWELL, 'Swiftsure', May 23, 1799'. Nelson was delighted, and for a while kept the coffin in his cabin, propped up behind his chair. He was buried in it on 8 January 1806.

SIXTY-SIX

Napoleon's toothbrush

The silver gilt handle engraved with a crown and monogram 'N' show this to be not just any old toothbrush. It was captured after Waterloo, when a Prussian major intercepted Napoleon's vast baggage train and sent the toothbrush to his wife as a novelty. The Wellcome Library confirms that Napoleon brushed his teeth regularly, 'using opium-based toothpaste', possibly without much effect, because (as Colin Jones reports in *The Smile Revolution*) Sir Henry Bunbury described his teeth as 'bad and dirty and he shows them very little'. On Saint Helena, adds Jones, they would soon be falling out.

SIXTY-SEVEN

Wellington's cavalry list

These cavalry numbers were totted up by the Duke of Wellington – shown here as the toast of London, covered in decorations – before the Battle of Waterloo on 18 June 1815. The methodical Duke listed 'Hussars, 1000; Vandeleurs, 1000; W[illiam] Ponsonby's, 1000; Grants, 1000; Household, 1000; Legion, 3091'. Below he added: 'Hanoverians, 1016; Hanoverians, lately arrived, 750; Brunswick Hussars, 750.' The total was 10,500 men. Later that day they would charge the French, capturing the two Eagles (the French battle standards) that would arrive in London on 21 June, poking out of a carriage window, but the toll was heavy. Ponsonby was killed, to Wellington's grief, and a captain in the Foot Guards later recorded the horror of facing a French cavalry charge: 'which, ever advancing, glittered like a stormy wave of the sea when it catches the sunlight. On they came until they got near enough, whilst the very earth seemed to vibrate…'

Hussars 1000 12 9
Vandeleurs 1000 12 9
Wm Ponsonby's 1000 12 9
Grants 1000 12 9
Household 1000 12 9
Legion 3091. 8000
Hanoverians 1016
Hanoverians lately arrived 750
Brunswick Hussars 750 10500
Cavalry – June 18 1815 – 2000
The above Computation in the Duke of Wellington's hand writing was given by His Grace To Sir John Elley Dy Adjutant General previous to the Battle of Waterloo

VITTORIA

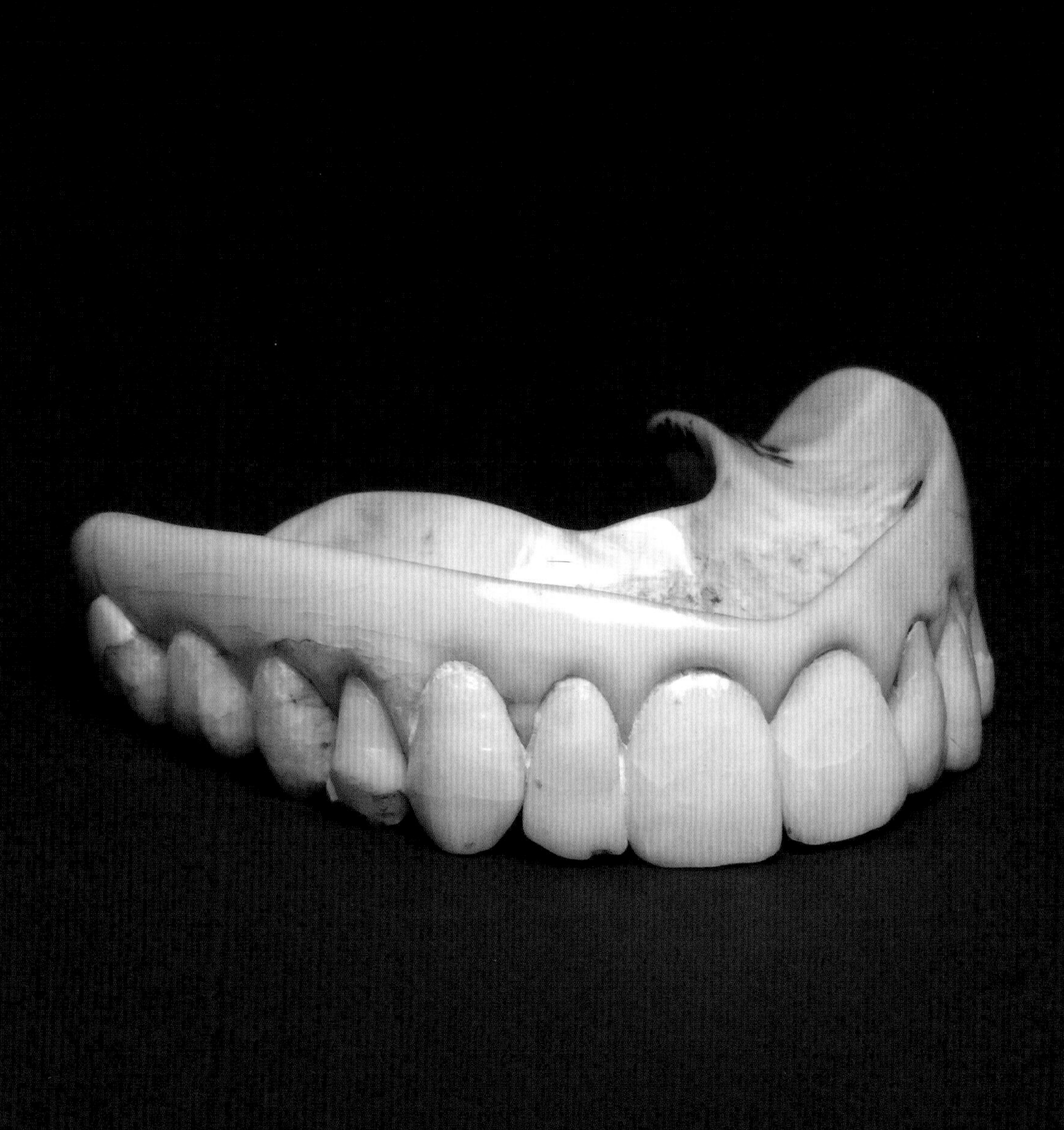

SIXTY-EIGHT

Waterloo Teeth

Every cloud has a silver lining, and many people made their fortunes selling the teeth taken from fallen soldiers after the Battle of Waterloo. So much so that real dentures, such as the handsome set shown here, were afterwards known as 'Waterloo Teeth', whether they hailed from that battlefield or not. Wellington himself lost his back teeth early in life and wore dentures, described by the historian Lucy Worsley as 'human teeth set into a jaw of animal bone or wood.' His son said, 'You may have observed that my father, when not speaking, had a movement of his lips, as if he were chewing,' going on to explain that the Duke's artificial teeth did not fit properly but without them his cheeks had a sunken look. 'It was only when he was compelled to wear a set of artificial teeth,' he added, 'that the natural configuration of his head returned.' This less-than-flattering sketch of Wellington was done at his deathbed, *sans* dentures. The Duke's own teeth are today on display at Apsley House, his London home.

SIXTY-NINE

Florence Nightingale's shoes

These soft beaded moccasins, perhaps imported from America, are said to have been worn by Florence Nightingale while nursing at Scutari during the Crimean War. Perhaps she wore them in the evenings: Mark Bostridge's *Florence Nightingale: The Woman and the Legend* explains that while 'she ordered the nurses' boots from Moore's in Knightsbridge, which sold servants' footwear, her own boots, with elastic sides rather than laces, came from Mr Chollocombe at Romsey, with galoshes to wear over them.' She would have needed the galoshes to work amid the blood and filth of nineteenth-century wartime nursing: one edition of *Notes on Nursing* even included a chapter on the 'Method of Polishing Floors' without water, as a way to keep the dirt to a minimum. As an interesting aside, one American journal of the era reported Florence's method of shoe selection as so: 'Miss Nightingale, despising the modern instrument of torture vended by fashionable shoemakers, is accustomed to plant her stocking foot firmly on a piece of leather, draw the outline of the figure it forms, and have her shoe made to correspond exactly with it!'

SEVENTY

Charles Darwin's walking stick

The great biologist and naturalist Charles Darwin used this walking stick late in life and considered it a *memento mori*; the skull, worn with use, is of whalebone – a nice link to his great journeys in the Southern oceans – and its eyes are glass. He took a short walk every day at 4 p.m., when his health allowed. His son later described the swinging action of his stick, which he struck against the ground as he walked in the gardens of Down House, his Kent home, making 'a rhythmical click which is with all of us a very distinct remembrance.' Walking was important throughout Darwin's life. In his autobiography he mentioned being once so absorbed in thought, as a young boy, that he walked right off an 8ft cliff. Of Cambridge, where he attended Christ's College, planning to study Divinity, he once remarked: 'I find Cambridge rather stupid, and I know scarcely any one that walks'. Eventually he found a walking companion: he took long strolls with Professor John Henslow, a clergyman, botanist and geologist.

SEVENTY-ONE

Murderers' death masks

This is a plaster copy of a death mask, made by pouring wax over head and face, cast from the corpse of James Bloomfield Rush. It may have been made by Tussauds, the famous firm begun by Frenchwoman Marie Grosholtz, who made wax death masks of the victims of the French Revolution and brought them to London. Rush wore a wig and fake whiskers to shoot a father and son on the steps of their mansion. The sketches show the mask of another notorious Victorian, the infamous Maria Manning, who murdered her wealthy lover with the help of her husband, burying him under the floor. Dickens attended their execution and was sickened by the crowd: 'thousands upon thousands of upturned faces,' he wrote, 'so inexpressibly odious in their brutal mirth and callousness.' Maria Manning inspired Hortense, the murderess in Dickens' *Bleak House*. These death masks and casts were of great interest to phrenologists, who sought clues to criminal leanings in the structure of the head.

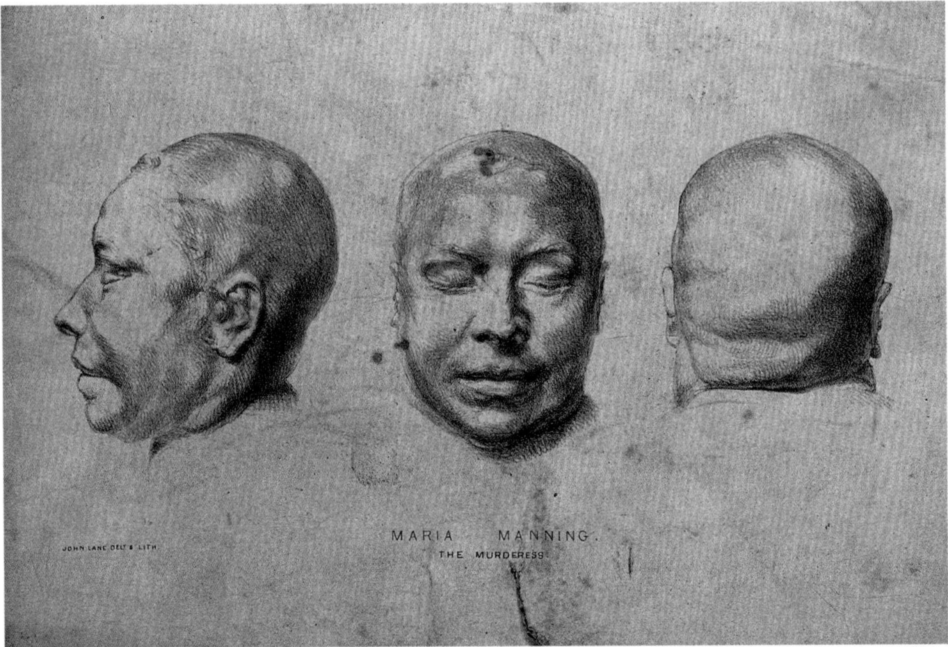

SEVENTY-TWO

A poisoner's cigar case

This pretty case contains a single unsmoked cigar, property of the man known as the 'Rugely Poisoner'. Dr William Palmer may have poisoned as many as seven people, including four of his own children, but was executed for the murder of a friend, John Parsons Cook, to whom he owed money. The pair went to the races: while Palmer lost on a horse called 'Chicken', Cook won a colossal £3,000. Afterwards they went for a drink and a smoke (perhaps from this very case) and, as they talked, Palmer gave his friend a glass of brandy and water. It tasted 'somewhat bad', Cook said, wondering aloud if there was 'something in it'. Cook later told a friend he thought Palmer might be 'dosing' him. He was right: Palmer finished him off a few days later, taking his betting book (filled with debts owed to Cook by Palmer) away with him, and using Cook's winnings to pay off some of his debts. Palmer was hanged on 14 June 1856, leaving us with the familiar pub phrase, 'What's your poison?'

SEVENTY-THREE

Gordon of Khartoum's last diary entry

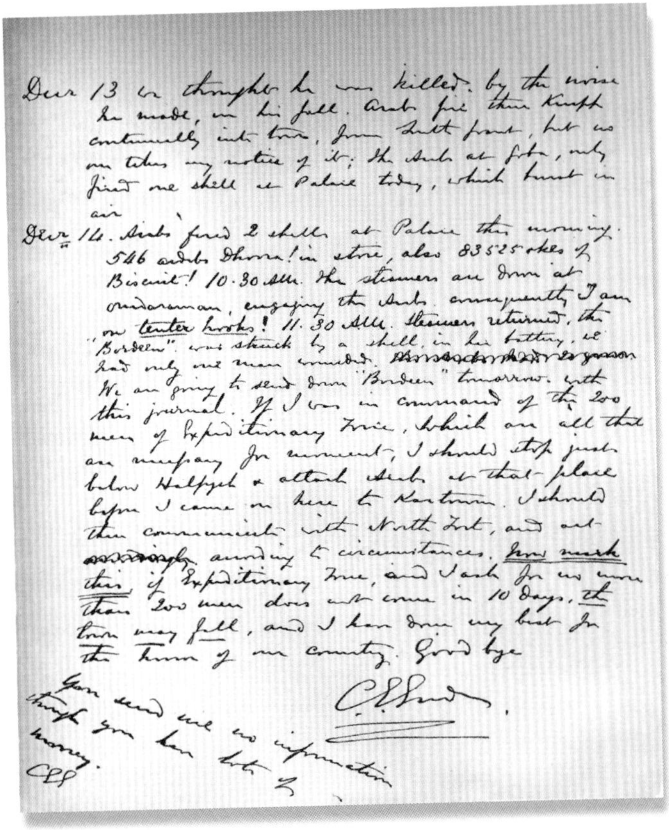
Dec 13 It is thought he was killed by the noise he made, in his fall. Arabs fire their Krupp continually into town, from South front, but no one takes any notice of it; the Arabs at Goba, only fired one shell at Palace today, which burst in air.

Dec 14. Arabs fired 2 shells at Palace this morning. 546 ardebs Dhoora! in store, also 83525 okes of Biscuit! 10.30 AM. The steamers are down at Omdurman, engaging the Arabs, consequently I am on tenter hooks! 11.30 AM. Steamers returned, the "Bordeen" was struck by a shell, in her battery, we had only one man wounded. [illegible] We are going to send down "Bordeen" tomorrow with this journal. If I was in command of the 200 men of Expeditionary Force, which are all that are necessary for movement, I should stop just below Halfyeh & attack Arabs at that place before I came on here to Kartoum. I should then communicate with North Fort, and act accordingly to circumstances. Now mark this, if Expeditionary Force, and I ask for no more than 200 men, does not come in 10 days, the town may fall, and I have done my best for the honour of our country. Good bye

C.G. Gordon

You send me no information though you have lots of money. CGG

In his time, Major General Charles George Gordon was as great a national hero as Nelson and Wellington. The general was already known as 'Chinese Gordon' for commanding the 'Ever-Victorious Army' during the Taiping Rebellion. He returned to Khartoum (where he had formerly governed, spending his days in failed attempts to crush the brutal slave trade) to evacuate British soldiers and citizens from the Sudan, which was in the grip of an uprising. Instead, he decided to hold the city against the rebels, and so began an extended siege. 'Now mark this,' he wrote in a final diary entry on 14 December 1884, 'if the Expeditionary Force … does not come in ten days, the town may fall, and I have done my best for the honour of my country. Goodbye.' In all he held the city for almost a year, perishing just two days before the Expeditionary Force arrived.

A620221
A620221
A620221

SEVENTY-FOUR

A Victorian surgeon's syringe set

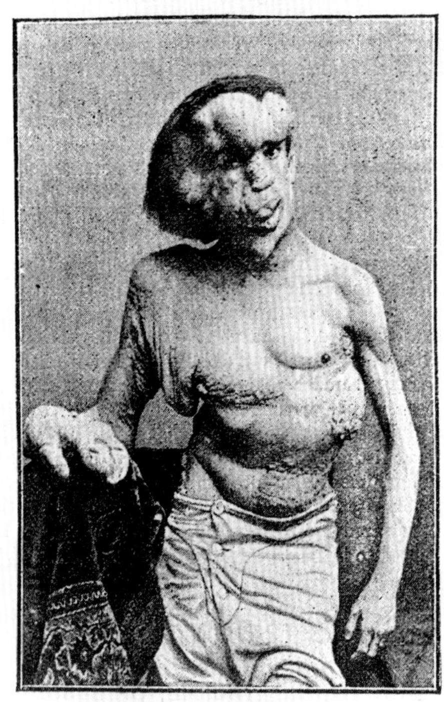

The "Elephant Man," from a photograph taken in 1889.

Sir Frederick Treves, a surgeon at the London Hospital and the owner of this syringe set, first saw Joseph Carey Merrick, 'The Elephant Man', half-naked in a Whitechapel shop in 1884. 'There stood revealed the most disgusting specimen of humanity that I have ever seen,' he wrote. Merrick could not speak. His skin smelt terribly. He was lame. Treves examined him at the hospital and gave him his card. Two years later, when police found Merrick robbed, starving and surrounded by a jeering mob in Liverpool Street station, the card was in his pocket. They became friends and Merrick, who probably suffered from neurofibromatosis or Proteus syndrome, became a social sensation: Alexandra, Princess of Wales, even sent him handwritten Christmas cards. He died at twenty-seven and Treves wrote movingly: 'As a specimen of humanity, Merrick was ignoble and repulsive; but the spirit of Merrick, if it could be seen in the form of the living, would assume the figure of an upstanding and heroic man, smooth browed and clean of limb, and with eyes that flashed undaunted courage.'

SEVENTY-FIVE

Charles Dickens' last letter

Charles Dickens was too busy to die: in this letter to his friend Charles Kent, written from Gad's Hill on 8 June 1870, he wrote, 'Tomorrow is a very bad day for me to make a call, as, in addition to my usual office business, I have a mass of accounts to settle … But I hope I may be ready for you at 3 o'clock. If I can't be – why, then, I shan't be.' That night, after a day spent working on his unfinished novel *Edwin Drood*, he suffered a stroke. As he staggered, his sister begged him to lie down: his last words were 'yes, on the ground'. He then passed out. He died the next day, having never regained consciousness. He wished to be buried in Kent, but public demand ensured a Westminster Abbey funeral. It was, however, secret: the grave was dug in Poets' Corner overnight and at 9.30 a.m. twelve family and friends attended alone. The grave remained open for two days thereafter so Londoners could pay their respects once the news broke.

Gad's Hill Place,
Higham by Rochester, Kent.

Wednesday Eighth June 1870

My dear Kent

Tomorrow is a very bad day for me to make a call, as, in addition to my usual office business, I have a mass of accounts to settle with Wills. But I hope I may be ready for you at 3 o'clock. If I can't be – why, then I shan't be.

You must really get rid of those Opal enjoyments. They are too overpowering:

"These violent delights have violent ends".

I think it was a father of your church who made the wise remark to a young gentleman who got up early (or stayed out late) at Verona?

Ever affectionately

CD

SEVENTY-SIX

Queen Victoria's dinner menu

Indefatigable diarist Queen Victoria was at Balmoral on 29 September 1897. 'Very dark, with a thick wet fog, but very mild,' she wrote, and described a hectic day of activity – saying goodbye to her grandson, seeing the doctor about her daughter-in-law's leg, going for a drive and having tea at Abergeldie – before visitors came to dine. This menu, created by her French chef, M. Ferry, perhaps goes some way to explaining the queen's 50-inch waist: it includes German potato soup, Normandy sole, fried whiting, grouse, roast beef, artichokes, and cold beef tongue on the side.

BALMORAL.

Her Majesty's Dinner
Wednesday 29 Septr 1897
Potages
Kartoffel Suppe
Consommé aux Quenelles
Poissons
Les Soles à la Normande
Les Merlans frits
Entrée
Croquettes de Grouse
Rélevé
Roast Beef [illegible]
Rôt
L'Oie
Entremêts
Les Artichauts Glacés
Babas au Curacoa
Mousseline de Pommes
Side table
Cold Fowl Cold Beef Tongue

SEVENTY-SEVEN

Lord Tennyson's *Idylls of the King*

This epilogue to the *Idylls of the King*, addressed to 'Her Majesty the Queen', was printed in 1872. Alfred Tennyson was by then a mature poet and there are just three corrections in this manuscript, but the *Idylls* itself – a twelve-poem cycle based on the romantic Arthurian legends – took over forty years to compose (some of it in the Hanbury Arms in Caerleon) and its success was the sweeter because he had known bitter failure in the past. He was so stung by criticism of his *Poems* (1832) that he couldn't publish for nearly ten years. But by the time he published this, he was Poet Laureate and would die a peer, leaving behind many popular poems and phrases such as ''Tis better to have loved and lost, than never to have loved at all.'

Original MS of the Epilogue to the "Idylls of the King": To the Queen.

O loyal to the royal in thyself,
And loyal to thy land, as this to thee—
Bear witness, that rememberable hour, morn
When pale from fever yet the goodly Prince,
Who scarce had pluck'd his flickering life again
From halfway down the shadow of the grave,
Past with thee thro' thy people & their love,
And London roll'd one ~~voice~~ tide of joy thro' all
Her trebled millions, & loud leagues of man
And welcome: witness too, the silent cry,
The prayer of many a people, creed & clime—
Thunderless lightnings striking under sea
From sunset & sunrise of all thy realm,
And that true North, whereof we lately heard
A strain to shame us 'Keep ye to yourselves,
[illegible] we sicken of your loyalty; ~~depart~~
Your love is as a burthen; get you gone!'
Is this the tone of empire? ~~faith in Him~~ this here the faith
That ~~Which~~ made us rulers? this, indeed, her voice
And meaning, whom the roar of Hougoumont
Left mightiest of all peoples in the west?
What shock has fool'd her since, that she should speak
So feebly? - wealthier - wealthier - hour by hour:
The voice of Britain, or a sinking land,
Some third-rate isle half-lost among her seas?
There rang her voice, when the full city peal'd
Thee & thy Prince! the loyal to their crown
Are loyal to their own far sons, who love
This ancient Ocean-empire, & her throne

SEVENTY-EIGHT

Newgate handcuffs

These iron handcuffs, stamped 'Newgate Prison', symbolize over 700 years of incarceration at the site above the long-buried Fleet River that is now London's Central Criminal Court, or the Old Bailey. Newgate was finally demolished in 1902. The prison appeared in Chaucer's *Canterbury Tales*, it burned in the Great Fire of London, was sprung during the Gordon Riots and held the last public execution in Britain. Famous prisoners included the novelist Daniel Defoe, the pirate Captain Kidd and the popular thief and gaol-breaker Jack Sheppard. Amelia Dyer the murderous 'baby-farmer' was hanged here, as was poisoner Dr Neil Cream. You can see the Victorian cells and hanging yard today, and the bell, in St Sepulchre's church opposite, that was rung outside the condemned cell before each execution.

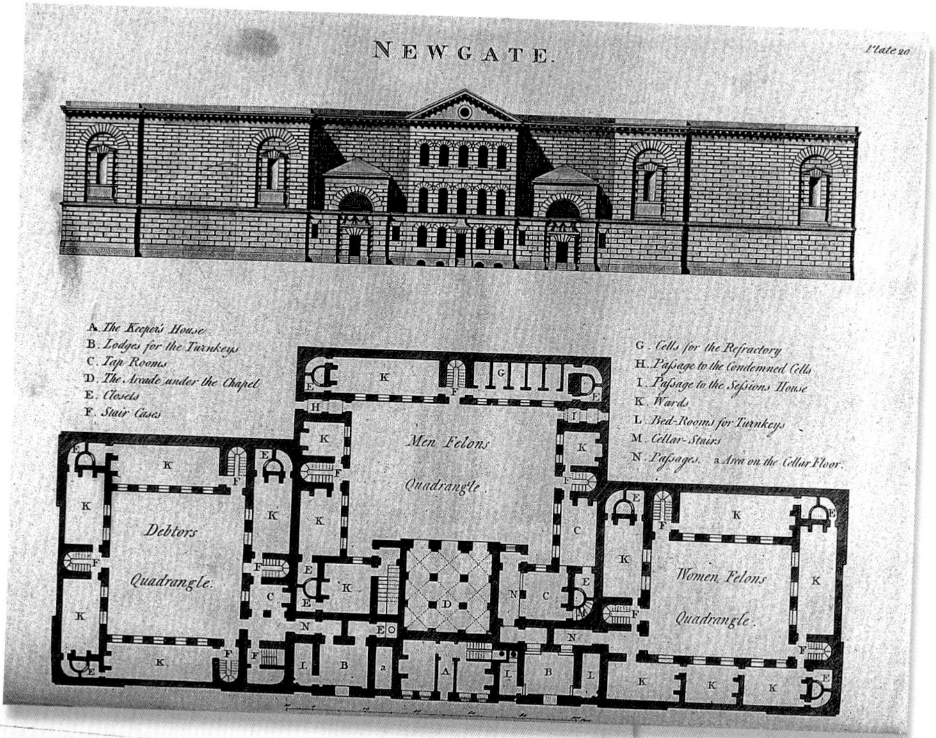

NEWGATE. Plate 20

A. The Keeper's House
B. Lodges for the Turnkeys
C. Tap Rooms
D. The Arcade under the Chapel
E. Closets
F. Stair Cases
G. Cells for the Refractory
H. Passage to the Condemned Cells
I. Passage to the Sessions House
K. Wards
L. Bed-Rooms for Turnkeys
M. Cellar-Stairs
N. Passages. a Area on the Cellar Floor.

Men Felons Quadrangle.

Debtors Quadrangle.

Women Felons Quadrangle.

SEVENTY-NINE

Lister's antiseptic spray

Joseph Lister, the pioneer of antiseptic surgery, was a Quaker who spent his honeymoon visiting hospitals and universities with his wife and research partner Agnes. His work at the University of Glasgow was based on Louis Pasteur's discovery of micro-organisms, refuting the belief that infections were carried in the air ('miasma') and asserting they could be destroyed by chemicals. Lister used this cumbersome 4.5kg apparatus ('like holding a baby hippo,' comments the Wellcome website) to spray carbolic acid on wounds, bandages and his surgical instruments and gown. He sprayed the air in the operating theatre, the nursing staff and patients. Survival rates soared by 15 per cent. King Edward VII, who collapsed with appendicitis two days before his coronation, directly credited Lister with his survival.

EIGHTY

Livingstone's medical case

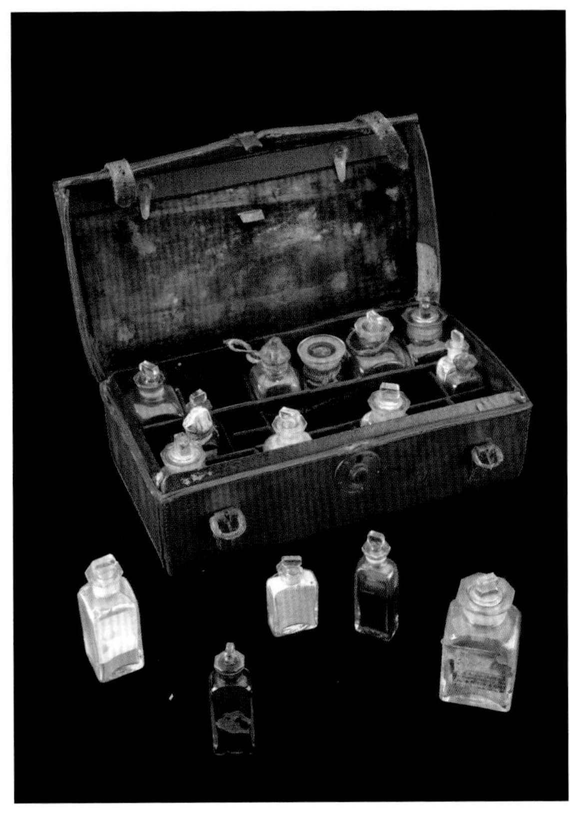

This collection of glass medicine bottles in a velvet-lined leather chest has quite a past. The Scottish explorer David Livingstone took it on his last trip down the River Nile, a journey immortalized by the words of American reporter H.M. Stanley: 'Dr Livingstone, I presume?' Livingstone had been missing for six years by the time that Stanley found him. The case still contains liquid ammonia (for treating snakebite), a lancet, a plaster, a brass weight and a caustic pencil. Stanley later sent Livingstone a second medicine case, as his medical supplies were constantly running out or being stolen. Livingstone's last act was to call for his medicine case, take out his bottle of calomel (mercurous chloride, used to induce vomiting) and say, 'All right; you can go out now.' He was found kneeling by his bed later that same night, quite dead. His African attendants buried his heart beneath a tree and carried his body 1,000 miles to the coast to be sent home. He is buried in Westminster Abbey.

EIGHTY-ONE

John Snow's medical diploma

University of London.

This is to Certify

that John Snow

obtained the Degree of Doctor of Medicine in this University at the Annual Examination for the same in the year 1844; and that he was placed in the First Division at the Pass Examination.

20. December 1844.

Burlington

Chancellor.

Dr John Snow, 'Father of Epidemiology', was the first person to realise that the cholera epidemics ravaging city populations were waterborne. His M.B. (Medicinae Baccalaureus) is dated 1844, but his breakthrough came ten years later, as he carefully mapped a cholera outbreak in the Soho parish of St James's. It centred on the Broad Street public water pump: of the eighty-three victims he tracked, three children had drunk directly from the pump, just near their school, others at a nearby pub (which used the water to water their spirits), and nine were customers of a local coffee shop. Snow suspected that the water had been contaminated with sewage (as it later proved). When the Parish Guardians took the handle off the pump, the outbreak slowed and Snow's work was used to improve London's sewage systems for decades to come.

EIGHTY-TWO

George Eliot's dedication

This charming dedication was written by the author Marian Evans, who wrote under the pseudonym George Eliot. *Adam Bede* was an enormous success and Evans gave due credit: 'To my dear husband, George Henry Lewes,' she wrote on 23 March 1859, 'I give this M.S. of a work which would never have been written but for the happiness which his love has conferred on my life.' The only fly in the ointment was that George was already married. Nevertheless, he and Evans lived together for twenty years and had three children, while his legal wife had four more with the editor of the *Daily Telegraph*. Despite the revelation of her scandalous home life, George Eliot continued to write best-selling books read by, among others, the prudish Queen Victoria, who declared them her favourites.

To my dear husband, George Henry Lewes,
I give this M.S. of a work which would
never have been written but for the
happiness which his love has conferred
on my life.

Marian Lewes.

March 23. 1859

The first volume was written at Richmond, the second at Munich & Dresden, the third at Richmond again. The work was begun on the 22nd October 1857, & finished on the 16th November 1858. A large portion of it was written twice: though often scarcely at all altered in the copying; but other parts only once, & among these the description of Dinah & a good deal of her sermon, the love scene between her & Seth, "Hetty's World", most of the scene in the Two Bedchambers, the talk between Arthur & Adam, various parts in the second volume which I can recall less easily, & in the third, Hetty's journeys, her confession & the cottage scenes.

EIGHTY-THREE

Queen Victoria's dancing shoes

One doesn't often think of the famously stout Queen Victoria dancing. This pair of ivory satin dancing slippers have sturdy leather soles, which were nailed on – but no heels. The petite Queen would therefore have attained a dancing height of just under 5ft, her arms just to the waist of a taller partner like Prince Albert. These shoes, in a then-fashionable style, were tied on with ribbons, like a modern ballet slipper. The soles have been worn down by their royal owner. Fascinatingly, the right shoe's seams are mismatched: the Queen wore poorly made dancing shoes. The shoe itself was lined with fine kid leather, and would have been soft to wear. The inside has a linen sock lining, with a sticker inside embossed with the Royal Arms. It reads 'GUNDRY & SON/ Boot & Shoe Makers/TO THE QUEEN/The Prince of Wales/THE ROYAL FAMILY/H.R.H THE DUCHESS OF KENT/and the/PRINCESS CHARLOTTE OF THE BELGIANS/1 Soho Square London'. The company made Victoria's shoes for nearly seventy-five years.

EIGHTY-FOUR

Prince Albert's waistcoat

This 'brown silk crepe single-breasted waistcoat embellished with blue embroidery' comes from the collection at the Museum of London. There is a button hidden in each lapel to ensure the jacket keeps a perfect line; a cinch at the back pulled it tight to Albert's trim figure. The embroidery is said to have been hand-worked by Prince Albert's third child Princess Alice. Embroidering Albert's clothes seems to have been somewhat of a family trait: Queen Victoria famously embroidered his cuffs with affectionate phrases. Princess Alice herself was a deeply sensitive soul. She befriended Florence Nightingale, and as an eighteen-year-old, cared for Queen Victoria's mother during her last days. In that same year, 1861, her father (still only forty-two) fell ill with what was then believed to be typhoid fever but is now thought to be, more probably, a terminal disease such as stomach cancer. He was cared for throughout his final illness by Princess Alice, who read to him for hours. Albert died at Windsor Castle at 10.50 p.m. on 14 December 1861, sending the whole nation into mourning. Princess Alice went to her wedding a few months afterwards in mourning black, changed into a white dress to wed, and immediately back into black once the vows were finalised; Queen Victoria (who wore black for the rest of her life) described it as 'more of a funeral than a wedding'. Alice too died young, at the age of just thirty-five: bending to kiss her son, who was ill, she caught the diphtheria infection that carried her off.

EIGHTY-FIVE

Edward Oxford's gun

Queen Victoria's survived eight assassination attempts. This pistol is one of two used by Edward Oxford, the first would-be assassin, an eighteen-year-old described in his indictment as 'a false traitor to our lady the Queen, who maliciously and traitorously, with force and arms, &c., did compass, imagine and intend to bring and put our said lady the Queen to death.' He paid £2 for the pair and practised in shooting galleries across London, opening fire as the Queen and Prince Albert rattled past the Green Park railings in their open coach. The first shot was heard to 'whiz by'; the Queen ducked and the second bullet missed. A passerby grabbed Oxford, taking his guns. 'You confounded rascal,' shouted someone in the crowd. 'How dare you shoot at our queen!' 'It was I,' said Oxford, and was immediately arrested. He spent the next twenty-four years in Bedlam and Broadmoor (despite being assessed as 'apparently sane'), then emigrated to Australia, married, and became a journalist – and a Church Warden to boot.

EIGHTY-SIX

Cellar murderer's letterhead

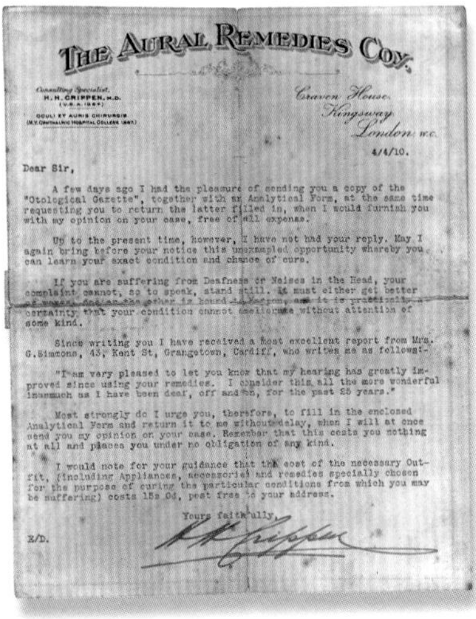

THE AURAL REMEDIES COY.

Consulting Specialist.
H. H. CRIPPEN, M.D.
(U.S.A. [illegible])
OCULI ET AURIS CHIRURGIS
(N.Y. OPHTHALMIC HOSPITAL COLLEGE [illegible])

Craven House.
Kingsway
London. W.C.

4/4/10.

Dear Sir,

A few days ago I had the pleasure of sending you a copy of the "Otological Gazette", together with an Analytical Form, at the same time requesting you to return the latter filled in, when I would furnish you with my opinion on your case, free of all expense.

Up to the present time, however, I have not had your reply. May I again bring before your notice this unexampled opportunity whereby you can learn your exact condition and chance of cure.

If you are suffering from Deafness or Noises in the Head, your complaint cannot, so to speak, stand still. It must either get better or worse, and as the other is bound to happen, [illegible] it is practically a certainty that your condition cannot ameliorate without attention of some kind.

Since writing you I have received a most excellent report from Mrs. G.Simmons, 43, Kent St, Grangetown, Cardiff, who writes me as follows:-

"I am very pleased to let you know that my hearing has greatly improved since using your remedies. I consider this all the more wonderful inasmuch as I have been deaf, off and on, for the past 25 years."

Most strongly do I urge you, therefore, to fill in the enclosed Analytical Form and return it to me without delay, when I will at once send you my opinion on your case. Remember that this costs you nothing at all and places you under no obligation of any kind.

I would note for your guidance that the cost of the necessary Outfit, (including Appliances, accessories and remedies specially chosen for the purpose of curing the particular conditions from which you may be suffering) costs 15s 0d, post free to your address.

Yours faithfully,

H H Crippen

E/D.

This letter to a prospective client from the 'Aural Remedies Co.' in London was sent by one of its 'consulting specialists', Dr Harvey Hawley Crippen, in April 1910. At the time he signed this letter his wife Cora had already been missing for two months, and the American homeopath was living openly with his mistress, Ethel Le Neve. Crippen, a hearing specialist, first met Ethel whilst working at a London institute for the deaf, and in this letter offers to send the client his 'opinion on your case, free of all charge'. Three months after this Edwardian equivalent of junk mail was sent, one of Cora's friends (Kate WIlliams, a professional strong-woman who went by the stage-name of 'Vulcana') filed a missing person's report, the police began to investigate the case, and Crippen and Ethel sailed for North America. The ship's captain contacted the police via wireless telegraph (its first such use): 'Strong suspicions that Crippen London cellar murderer and accomplice are among saloon passengers. Mustache taken off growing beard. Accomplice dressed as boy. Manner and build undoubtedly a girl.' The pair were arrested on board: he was hanged at Pentonville in November; she was acquitted, and died in Croydon in 1967.

EIGHTY-SEVEN

Shackleton's snow goggles

Ernest Shackleton must have looked terrifying wearing these primitive snow goggles in the dazzling whiteness of his 1907-09 South Pole *Nimrod* expedition. He had two pairs, one of which was discarded because it restricted ventilation, both with coloured glass lenses to reduce snow blindness. Shackleton's tiny notebook documents their gruelling attempt on the South Pole, hampered by bad feeling among his team, the *Nimrod* itself (their ship, which was 'much dilapidated and smelt strongly of seal oil') and an unusual diet that included minced penguin liver. All four of his ponies died during the attempt: the four men pulled their own sledges almost 100 miles to the Pole and back, returning unsuccessful and in skeletal condition ('we are so thin that our bones ache as we lie on the hard snow in our sleeping bags, from which a great deal of the hair is gone,' he wrote in *Heart of the Antarctic*). They caught their ship home by a whisker, earning a place in the history of exploration and a knighthood for Shackleton.

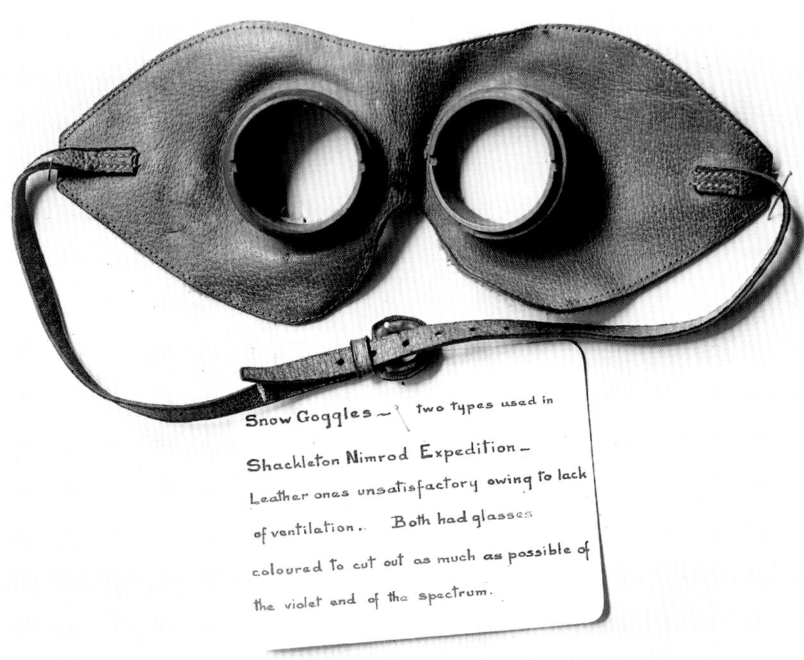
Snow Goggles – two types used in
Shackleton Nimrod Expedition –
Leather ones unsatisfactory owing to lack
of ventilation.. Both had glasses
coloured to cut out as much as possible of
the violet end of the spectrum.

we shall stick it out
to the end but we
are getting weaker of
course and the end
cannot be far.
It seems a pity but
I do not think I can
write more –
R. Scott
Last Entry
For Gods sake look
after our people

EIGHTY-EIGHT

Scott's diary

For sheer stiff-upper-lip heroism and dignified courage, the diary kept by Robert Falcon Scott on his *Terra Nova* expedition of 1910-1913 reigns supreme. Scott reached the South Pole, where this picture was taken, as Shackleton did not – only to find the Norwegian team had got there first. The dog teams and supplies they expected never arrived, the frostbitten Captain Oates walked out into the snow to his death ('I am just going outside and may be some time') to avoid delaying his friends, and storms set in. The whole team died in tents pitched just 11 miles from their supply depot. Scott wrote this message on 29 March 1912, most probably the day on which he died: 'We shall stick it out to the end, but we are getting weaker, of course, and the end cannot be far. It seems a pity, but I do not think I can write any more. R. Scott. For God's sake look after our people.' The team were finally reached – and buried – in November.

King Edward VII's body

This photograph shows the body of King Edward VII, the once-portly, racing-mad son of Queen Victoria. He remained on his deathbed for eight days as his funeral was arranged. It took place on 20 May 1910 and was one of the largest gatherings of European royalty ever seen. The king's German cousin, Kaiser Wilhelm II, marched in the funeral procession; four years later the two countries would be at war, many of the nine monarchs following the cortege would lose their crowns and the Archduke Franz Ferdinand of Austria (also at the funeral) would be assassinated, triggering the outbreak of war. The king's last words were 'I am very glad', said to be on hearing that his horse had won at Kempton Park. Royal Ascot went ahead, minus the royal party and in full mourning, and was known ever after as 'Black Ascot'.

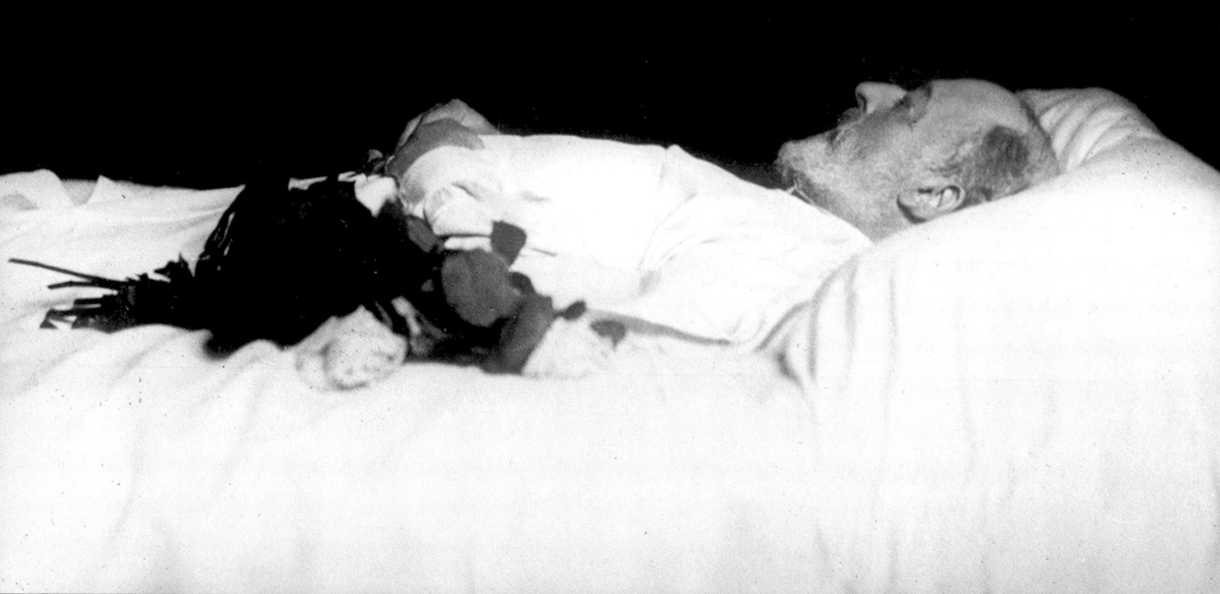

NINETY

King Edward VII's favourite dog

King Edward VII's dog Caesar, the wire-haired fox terrier seen in this photographer, broke the hearts of the nation by walking behind the king's favourite horse at his funeral. Bred by the Duchess of Newcastle (later President of the Wire Fox Terrier Association), he was also the author of bestseller *Where's Master?* Sir John Ernest Hodder-Williams, its ghost-writer and, coincidentally, chairman of publisher Hodder and Stoughton, went straight for the jugular: 'Where's Master?', it begins, 'I've been hunting for him high and low for days. I can't find Master anywhere, and I'm so lonely.' In the book, Caesar reminisced about his life with the king and his last moments by his bedside, ending with the king's funeral. 'We've come to the end of the journey,' the book concludes. 'They say there are no little dogs where Master has gone. But I know better...'

NINETY-ONE

Report on the sinking of the *Titanic*

This report was written by Arthur Henry Rostron, captain of the RMS *Carpathia*, which rescued many *Titanic* survivors. Writing twelve days after the disaster he described the urgent wireless distress signal saying she had struck ice and needed immediate assistance. The *Carpathia* switched off her heating systems to get there faster, reaching the stricken ship around 4 a.m. 'The night was beautifully fine but cold,' he remembered, describing the green distress flares as 'Roman Candles throwing out stars'. He avoided dozens of icebergs 'large + small' to carry the 700 survivors to New York, where relatives and well-wishers waited in the rain. Survivors included (controversially) Bruce Ismay, Managing Director of the White Star Line, which owned the *Titanic*. John Jacob Astor IV escorted his pregnant eighteen-year-old wife to safety and then went down with the ship. Another millionaire, Benjamin Guggenheim, did the same and was last seen smoking a cigar with his valet as the ship sank. 'We've dressed up in our best,' he was heard to say, 'and are prepared to go down like gentlemen.' His mistress, also on board, survived the disaster.

RMS Carpathia
Cunard SS Co Ltd
At Sea
April 27th 1912

At 12.35 am (ships time) April 15th Monday, 1912, I was called by the 1st officer in company with Marconi operator + informed that the White Star Line RMS Titanic was sending out urgent distress signals by wireless, that she had struck ice + required immediate assistance also giving position of Titanic as Lat 41°46 N Long 50°14 W

I immediately ordered the Carpathia turned round sent for the Chief Engineer, made out course + found we were then S52°W (true), 58 miles from Titanic also sent wireless to Titanic saying we were coming to her assistance.

The Carpathia was then on a voyage from New York to Mediterranean ports, with passengers mail + cargo

I gave Chief Engineer instructions to turn out another watch of stokers + to make all speed possible

I then ordered all our boats prepared + swung out ready for lowering. Interviewed the head officials of each department giving them all instructions I considered necessary to meet any emergency, + had all hands called.

The night was beautifully fine but cold

At 2.40 am saw green flare up half a point on port bow (White Star Line Co's signal stating this to be the ship) I immediately had rockets fired in answer, having previously given orders to fire rockets at 3 am + each quarter hour after.

A few minutes after seeing the flare up we saw our first ice berg, (having to alter course several times from then on until our arrival on scene of disaster) to avoid icebergs.

We kept good bearings of the flare ups which was shown about every quarter of an hour [illegible] + answered with rockets + also with Cunard Co's night signals (Roman Candles throwing out stars)

At 4 am stopped the ship + abt 4.10 am got first boat alongside the ship with officer in charge

By the time the first boat was cleared it was breaking day, we could then see we were surrounded by ice bergs large + small + later saw extensive field ice [illegible]

On the officer coming aboard he reported Titanic [illegible]

NINETY-TWO

Emmeline Pankhurst's shoe

This tiny shoe, described by the Museum of London as a 'black kid leather court shoe with small curved heel, decorated with a black satin rosette and black beadwork' flew off in one of Emmeline Pankhurst's struggles with the police. The Suffragette leader was not an easy woman to arrest, defended as she was by a thirty-strong gang of women nicknamed 'the Amazons', who were trained by a fellow Suffragist called Edith Margaret Garrud (one of the first female martial-arts trainers in Britain). Edith's style of defence – throwing policemen over her shoulder, in one well-publicized example – was captured in a 1907 Pathé film (now sadly lost) called *Jiu-Jitsu Downs the Footpads.* Even when arrested, 'Emmeline' often turned out to be a decoy, such as another woman wearing her clothes. This 1908 photograph shows Mrs Pankhurst reading the paper with her daughter Christabel while in hiding on a roof at Clements Inn. Emmeline's toughness was legendary: she once kept warders out of her prison cell with nothing but a water jug, crying, 'If any of you dares so much as to take one step inside this cell I shall defend myself'. They retreated.

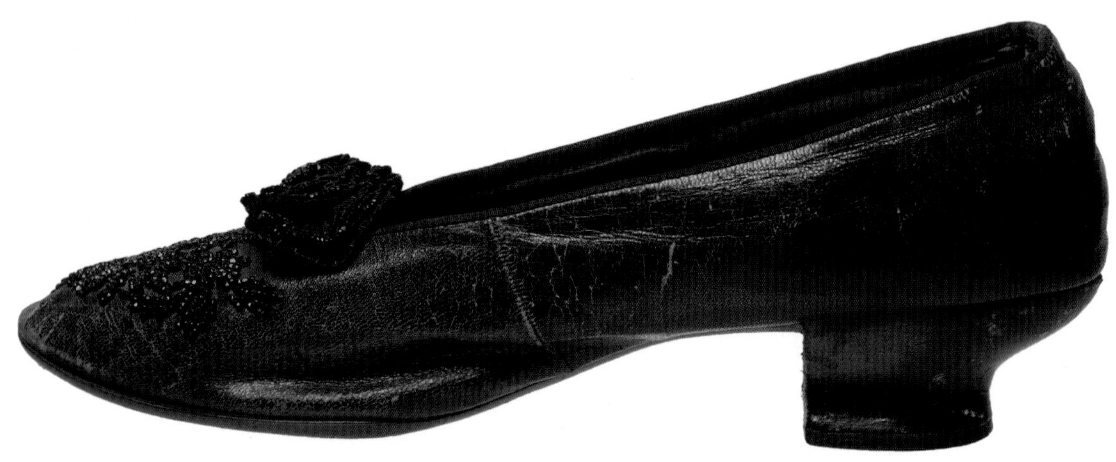

0315

L. B. & S. C. Ry.

4th JUNE 1913.

Available this DAY only.

EPSOM RACE COURSE to

Victoria

No particular class of carriage guaranteed.

FARE. 8s. 6d.

See conditions on back.

NINETY-THREE

Emily Wilding Davison's return ticket

On the left of this horrifying photograph is the Suffragette Emily Wilding Davison falling under the feet of the king's horse, Anmer, during the Derby at Epsom racecourse. She died four days later, on 8 June 1913: the jockey, Herbert Jones, laid a wreath at her funeral. The return ticket to Victoria found in her purse raised questions about her true purpose: she may have been trying to attach something to the horse at what was then the most famous flat race in the world. Wilding went to prison nine times during her Suffrage career. She was force-fed, and once threw herself from a gangway in Holloway in protest at the horrific treatment of Suffragists. On her coffin was written 'Deeds not Words', the slogan of the Women's Social and Political Union (WSPU); she was buried wearing her Suffrage medals.

NINETY-FOUR

First World War tank mask

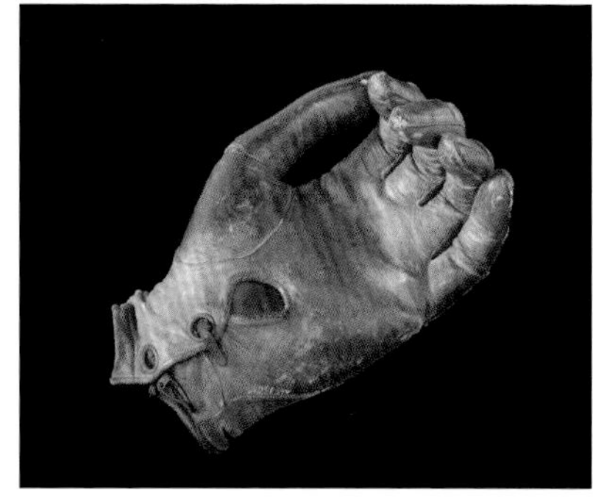

These sinister accessories were used by British soldiers, or 'Tommies', in the First World War, and reveal some unusual aspects of that conflict. The protective mask was worn by tank crews in the 'land ships' partly designed by a thirty-something Winston Churchill. Despite the conflict being the first 'modern' war, deploying machine-guns, artillery, chemical weapons and aeroplanes, the brutal day-to-day reality could be almost medieval: hand-to-hand combat with weapons that included improvised maces (wooden clubs with nails hammered through), knives, and 'French Nail' knuckledusters like these. The horrific injuries caused by these weapons, and even more so by the rounds, shells and explosives the troops were subjected to, forced medical science to take huge leaps forward. However, this artificial limb – encased in a glove to make it more realistic – is of a design familiar from Ambrose Paré's Tudor prosthesis. Many other First World War amputees had to make do with simple steel hooks.

NINETY-FIVE

The first asthma inhalers

Edwardian asthmatics rushed to buy this 'pipe of peace', packaged with a swan-necked glass tube inhaler to calm the breathing using warm-water vapour and a drug called 'Dirigin'. Pipe and drug were the brainchild of an American inventor, Hiram Maxim, who later became a British citizen and was famous for inventing the less peaceful machine gun. According to the *New York Times*, Maxim met a fellow American in Vienna in 1882 who advised him: 'Hang your chemistry and electricity! If you want to make a pile of money, invent something that will enable these Europeans to cut each others' throats with greater facility!' His gun fired 600 rounds a minute, growing so red-hot that the gunners had to urinate on the barrel to cool it. Hilaire Belloc summed up its destructive powers in this pithy couplet: 'Whatever happens, we have got / The Maxim gun, and they have not.'

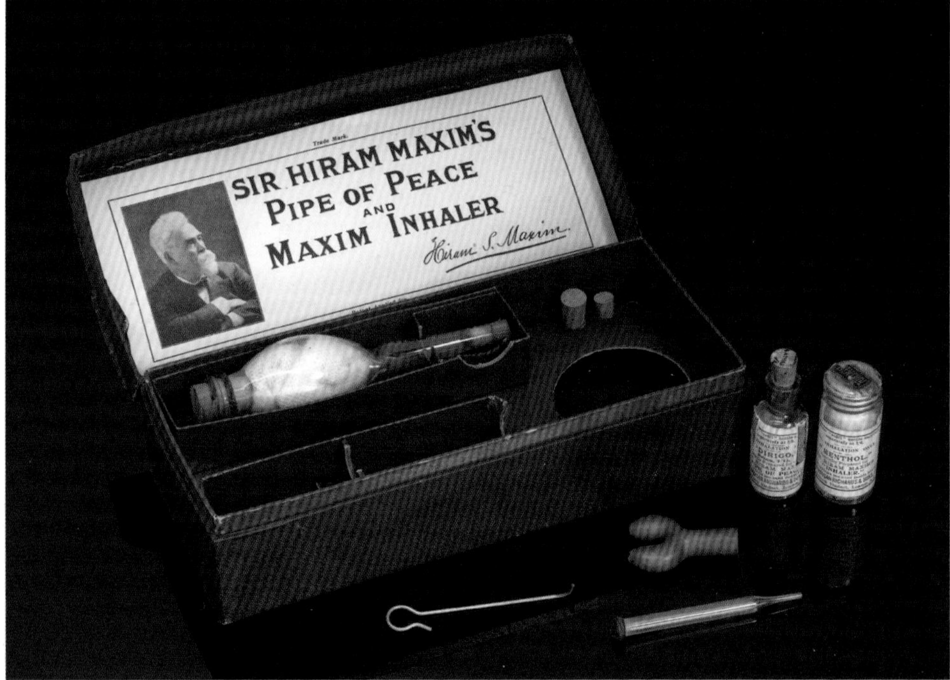

NINETY-SIX

Zeppelin photograph

The first Zeppelin raid on Britain took place in January 1915. This extraordinary image, like something from the ocean, was taken by an amateur in early September 1915 and published by *The Illustrated London News* as: 'An Untouched[-up] Photograph of A Zeppelin Raiding the London District – As Thousands of People Saw It'. The magazine explained that because the image was taken at night there was 'no great detail … however, it gives a very excellent impression of one of the hostile aircraft over the London district during the raid'. Count von Zeppelin first became interested in flight while fighting in the American Civil War. At this early stage, Zeppelin crews simply leant over the side to drop munitions by hand.

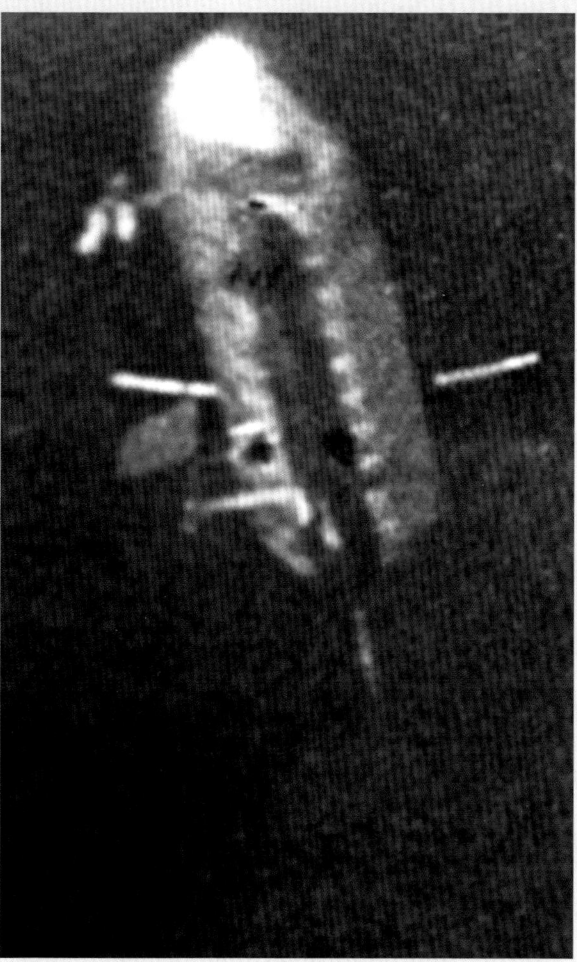

NINETY-SEVEN

Christmas card from a British concentration camp

Alexandra Palace, the Victorian 'People's Palace' in Haringey, North London, became the Palace Camp for German civilian prisoners during the First World War. The cheery image in this Christmas and New Year card, sent in 1915, its first year of opening, belies the tough conditions inside. About 3,000 men, women and children, many of them English, slept on plank beds like the one pictured here. Simon Webb's history of British concentration camps reveals that one of the main causes of complaint was the buckets: the same ones were used for cleaning the floors and serving up the soup. By the end of the war the inmates were eating horse meat and subsisting on 1,500 calories a day, leaving them little energy to use the gym and sports fields provided.

NINETY-EIGHT

Armistice Telegram

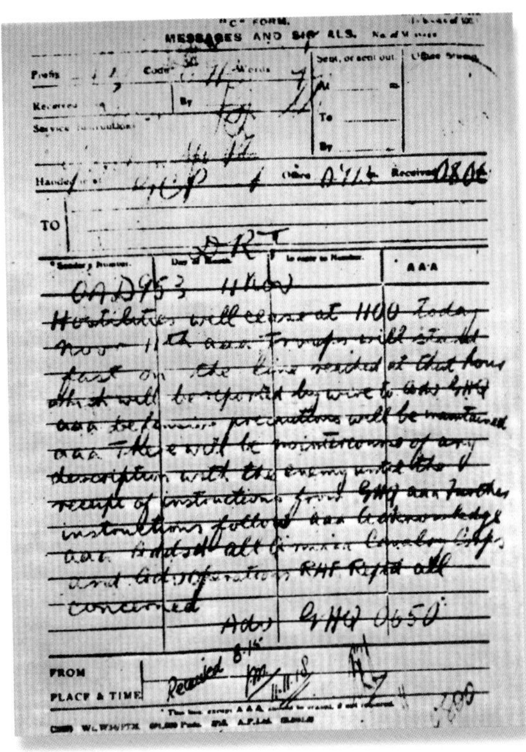

"C" FORM.
MESSAGES AND SIGNALS.

Prefix | Code | Words
Received | By
Service Instructions
Handed in at | Office | Received 0806

TO

Sender's Number | Day of Month | In reply to Number | AAA

OAD 953 11 Nov

Hostilities will cease at 1100 today Nov 11th aaa Troops will stand fast on the line reached at that hour which will be reported by wire to GHQ aaa Defensive precautions will be maintained aaa There will be no intercourse of any description with the enemy until the receipt of instructions from GHQ aaa Further instructions follow aaa Acknowledge aaa Addsd all Armies Cavalry Corps and [illegible] RAF Repd all concerned

GHQ 0650

FROM
PLACE & TIME
Received 8.15 11.11.18

This is the telegram that everyone was waiting for in 1918. 'Hostilities will cease at 1100 on Nov 11,' reads the faded text of the Armistice Telegram. 'Troops will stand fast on the time reached at that hour which will be reported by wire to GHQ.' It was dated 11-11-18. In an Imperial War Museum podcast, William Davies of the Machine Gun Corps recalls seeing the news in Paris and telling his sceptical unit. 'I got back … and said "This war's nearly over" and they would not believe me. They said it was absolutely ridiculous – not in that language …' But it was true. The accord was signed at 5 a.m., and by 11 a.m. the four-year 'war to end all wars' was finally over. Many of the men at the front reported feeling only relief mixed with exhaustion, but places like London went absolutely wild with joy. Winston Churchill was in his Whitehall office when the war ended: 'Then suddenly, the first stroke of the chime. I looked again at the broad street beneath me – it was deserted. Then, from all sides men and women came scurrying into the street. Streams of people poured from all the buildings. The bells of London began to clash. Northumberland Avenue was now crowded with hundreds, nay, thousands rushing hither and thither in a frantic manner shouting and screaming with joy.'

NINETY-NINE

The Versailles' table

On 28 June 1919 a gun salute outside the Palace of Versailles marked the signing of the treaty that ended the First World War. The momentous occasion took place in the famous Hall of Mirrors, on the table shown in this photograph. Harold Nicholson, the writer and diplomat, described the scene that day, with the press at one end of the hall, hundreds of seats for delegates in the middle and at the other end, 'like a guillotine … the table for the signatures.' Germany was not party to the negotiations, but her officials were the first of twenty-one countries to sign. 'The silence is terrifying,' wrote Nicholson, 'They [the Germans] are deathly pale.' It was the fifth anniversary of Franz Ferdinand's assassination. Gavrilo Princip's first bullet hit the Archduke, the second his wife. His last words to her were reportedly, 'Sophie, Sophie! Don't die! Live for our children!' Clemenceau closed the day with some of the most anti-climatic words in history: '"*La seance est levee*" [the meeting is adjourned] rasped Clemenceau,' recorded Nicholson. 'Not a word more or less. We kept our seats while the Germans were conducted like prisoners from the dock, their eyes still fixed upon some distant point of the horizon.'

ONE HUNDRED

Edward VIII's letter of abdication

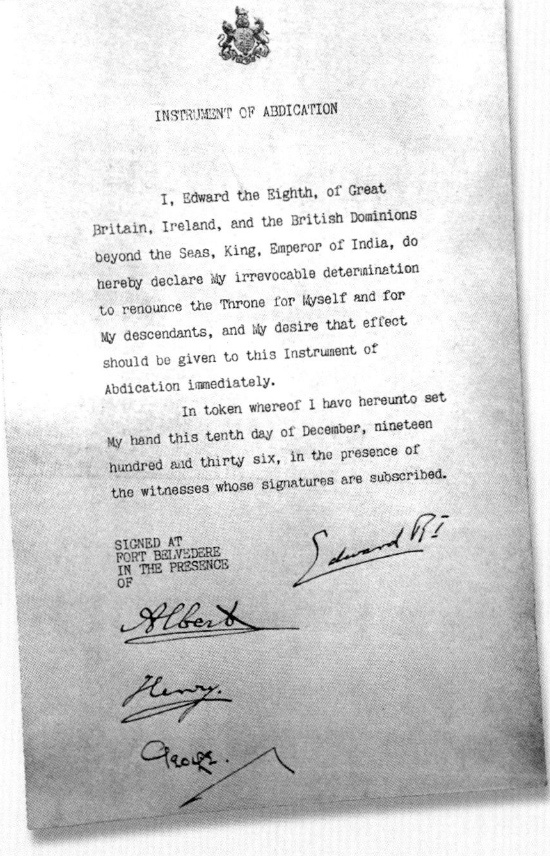

INSTRUMENT OF ABDICATION

I, Edward the Eighth, of Great Britain, Ireland, and the British Dominions beyond the Seas, King, Emperor of India, do hereby declare My irrevocable determination to renounce the Throne for Myself and for My descendants, and My desire that effect should be given to this Instrument of Abdication immediately.

In token whereof I have hereunto set My hand this tenth day of December, nineteen hundred and thirty six, in the presence of the witnesses whose signatures are subscribed.

SIGNED AT
FORT BELVEDERE
IN THE PRESENCE
OF

Edward RI

Albert

Henry.

George.

Many souvenirs, from tie pins to china cups, still exist for the coronation that never happened, all marked 12 May 1937. But in December 1936 the dashing King Edward VIII, who acceded that year on his father's death, relinquished his throne to marry the American divorcee Wallis Simpson. The terse, typed document is signed 'Edward R' ('Rex' for 'King') and the co-signatories are three of his brothers. The man who was now to become King George VI, father of Queen Elizabeth II, used his real name, Albert. It was signed at Fort Belvedere, where Edward had lived riotously as Prince of Wales ('What could you possibly want that queer old place for? Those damn weekends, I suppose,' his father George V is supposed to have said), adding a swimming pool, tennis court, bathrooms, steam-room and central heating. He spent his first weekend with Wallis there in 1932 and she was there until a week before the Abdication. They never lived there again. Only Lady Jane Grey, the 'Nine Day Queen', had a shorter reign on the English throne than Edward VIII; she was beheaded in 1554.

ONE HUNDRED AND ONE

DNA Nobel prize telegram

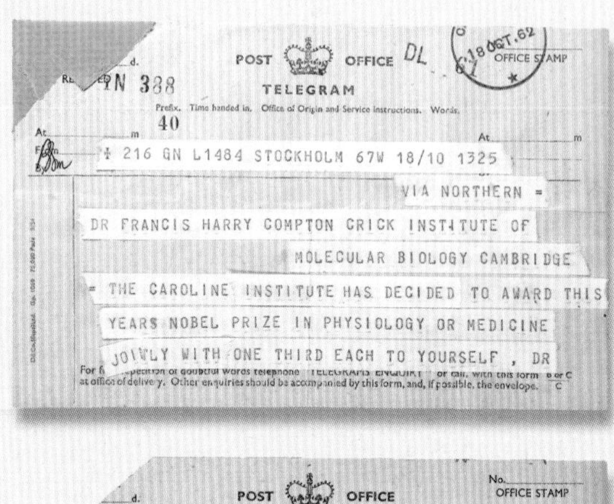

POST OFFICE TELEGRAM

OFFICE STAMP 18 OCT.62

N 388

40

+ 216 GN L1484 STOCKHOLM 67W 18/10 1325

VIA NORTHERN =

DR FRANCIS HARRY COMPTON CRICK INSTITUTE OF

MOLECULAR BIOLOGY CAMBRIDGE

= THE CAROLINE INSTITUTE HAS DECIDED TO AWARD THIS

YEARS NOBEL PRIZE IN PHYSIOLOGY OR MEDICINE

JOINTLY WITH ONE THIRD EACH TO YOURSELF , DR

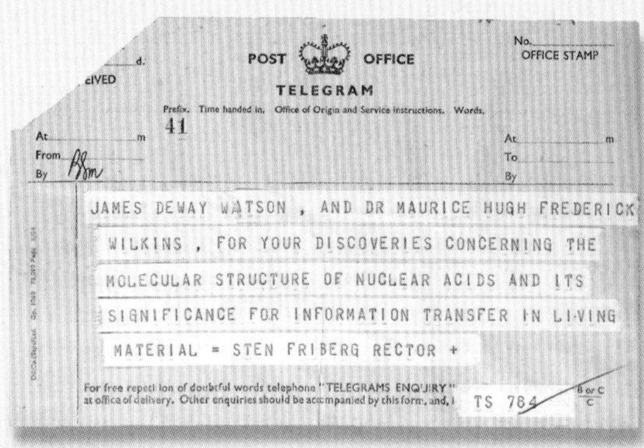

POST OFFICE TELEGRAM

OFFICE STAMP

41

JAMES DEWAY WATSON , AND DR MAURICE HUGH FREDERICK

WILKINS , FOR YOUR DISCOVERIES CONCERNING THE

MOLECULAR STRUCTURE OF NUCLEAR ACIDS AND ITS

SIGNIFICANCE FOR INFORMATION TRANSFER IN LIVING

MATERIAL = STEN FRIBERG RECTOR +

For free repetition of doubtful words telephone "TELEGRAMS ENQUIRY" at office of delivery. Other enquiries should be accompanied by this form, and,

TS 784

This eight-line telegram, sent on 18 October 1962 from the Karolinska Institute in Stockholm, was so momentous it had to be split in two. It told the Cambridge-based molecular biologist Francis Crick (aged forty-six) he had won the Nobel Prize in Physiology or Medicine for his work on the double-helix structure of DNA. In fact he won a third of the prize, sharing it with New Zealand-born Maurice Wilkins (forty-five) and the American James Watson (thirty-four), for 'discoveries concerning the molecular structure of nuclear [*sic*] acids and its significance for information transfer in living material'. A fourth scientist was left out of the citation, the brilliant X-Ray crystallographer Rosalind Franklin, who died before the prize was awarded. Watson fell into reduced circumstances after the award, and was forced to sell his medal (raising just over $4 million) in 2014. It was bought by a Russian multi-billionaire, who kindly returned it to him.

Image Credits

1. Science Museum, London and Wellcome Images
2. Science Museum, London and Wellcome Images
3. British Library, Cotton Nero C. IV, f.39
4. British Library, Cotton Vitellius A. XV, f.132 and Gallimaufry, Shutterstock
5. British Library, Add. 4838; 5b: British Library, Cotton Augustus II.106
6. Wellcome Library, London and British Library, Royal 20 A.II f.5
7. © National Portrait Gallery, London
8. 8. British Library, Add. 10302, f.37v.jpg
9. Reproduced courtesy of the Dean and Chapter of Canterbury
10. Science Museum, London, Wellcome Images
11. British Library, Cotton Nero D. IV, f.25v
12. Science Museum, London, Wellcome Images
13. Publisher's collection; (portrait) British Library, 167.c.26, frontispiece
14. Science Museum, London, Wellcome Images and British Library, Lansdowne 451, f.127
15. © Dean and Chapter of Westminster
16. Facsimiles of Royal, Historical, and Literary Autographs in the British Museum and The Duke in the Tower of London in 1500 (British Library, Royal 16 F. II, f.73)
17. British Library, Add MS 18850 f256v
18. Science Museum, London, Wellcome Images
19. British Library, Stowe Charter 617
20. British Library, Royal 2 A. XVI, f.63v
21. 21. Facsimiles of Royal, Historical, and Literary Autographs in the British Museum and Everett Historical, Shutterstock
22. Facsimiles of Royal, Historical, and Literary Autographs in the British Museum and Wellcome Library, London
23. British Library, Stowe 956
24. British Library, c27e19
25. Facsimiles of Royal, Historical, and Literary Autographs in the British Museum and Pictures of English History
26. Facsimiles of Royal, Historical, and Literary Autographs in the British Museum
27. Science Museum, London, Wellcome Images
28. British Library, bishop's bible BLF G.12188, title page
29. Science Museum, London, Wellcome Images
30. Facsimiles of Royal, Historical, and Literary Autographs in the British Museum and Sketch of the Trial of Mary Queen of Scots, British Library, Add. 48027, f.569*
31. Facsimiles of Royal, Historical, and Literary Autographs in the British Museum
32. British Library, Royal 7 D. X, binding and Everett Historical / Shutterstock
33. Science Museum, London, Wellcome Images and Wellcome Library, London
34. Science Museum, London, Wellcome Images
35. British Library, HMNTS 9510. bbb.11, Wellcome Library, London V0041786. and British Library, 001394795
36. Courtesy of the Virginia Historical Society Courtesy, 1953.4.A-B and Library of Congress, LC-USZ62-8104.
37. British Library, Egerton 1787 and (folio) British Library, F G.11631, title page
38. Facsimiles of Royal, Historical, and Literary Autographs in the British Museum
39. Museum of London, ID no: A27050
40. Publisher's collection
41. Wellcome Library, London
42. Museum of London
43. Fanshawe's and the King's recipes, Wellcome Library, London; contemporary wax plague scene, Science Museum, London, Wellcome Images
44. Publisher's collection
45. Facsimiles of Royal, Historical, and Literary Autographs in the British Museum
46. Deminsteriman, Shutterstock
47. Facsimiles of Royal, Historical, and Literary Autographs in the British Museum

48. Wellcome Library, London and Everett Historical, Shutterstock
49. Facsimiles of Royal, Historical, and Literary Autographs in the British Museum
50. Facsimiles of Royal, Historical, and Literary Autographs in the British Museum
51. Library of Congress, LC-USZ61-922
52. Wellcome Library, London and Publisher's collection
53. Facsimiles of Royal, Historical, and Literary Autographs in the British Museumand Wellcome Library, London
54. Facsimiles of Royal, Historical, and Literary Autographs in the British Museum
55. British Library, Ashley 5022, binding
56. Science Museum, London, Wellcome Images
57. Science Museum, London, Wellcome Images
58. Science Museum, London, Wellcome Images and Wellcome Library, London
59. Wellcome Library, London
60. Facsimiles of Royal, Historical, and Literary Autographs in the British Museum
61. Wellcome Library, London and Science Museum, London, Wellcome Images
62. Wellcome Library, London
63. Facsimiles of Royal, Historical, and Literary Autographs in the British Museum
64. Wellcome Library, London
65. Publisher's collection
66. Science Museum, London, Wellcome Images
67. Facsimiles of Royal, Historical, and Literary Autographs in the British Museum
68. Science Museum, London, Wellcome Images
69. Wellcome Library, London
70. Science Museum, London, Wellcome Images
71. Science Museum, London, Wellcome Images
72. Science Museum, London, Wellcome Images
73. Facsimiles of Royal, Historical, and Literary Autographs in the British Museum
74. Science Museum, London, Wellcome Images (and photo, Wellcome Library, London)
75. Facsimiles of Royal, Historical, and Literary Autographs in the British Museum and (sketch) Wellcome Library, London
76. Wellcome Library, London
77. Facsimiles of Royal, Historical, and Literary Autographs in the British Museum
78. Science Museum, London, Wellcome Images and Wellcome Library, London
79. Science Museum, London, Wellcome Images
80. Science Museum, London, Wellcome Images
81. Wellcome Library, London
82. Facsimiles of Royal, Historical, and Literary Autographs in the British Museum
83. Museum of London
84. Metropolitan Police
85. Wellcome Library, London
86. Wellcome Library, London
87. Publisher's collection; Science Museum, London, Wellcome Images and Library of Congress, LC-USZ62-8744
88. Library of Congress, LC-DIG-ggbain-08176
89. Publisher's collection
90. Library of Congress, LC-USZ62-64157, plus Everett Historical, Shutterstock
91. Publisher's collection and LSE Library, 7JCC/O/02/121
92. LSE, 1913-06-04 7EWD/M/30ITEM and LSE, TWL/2004/321
93. Science Museum, London, Wellcome Images
94. Science Museum, London, Wellcome Images and Olemac, Shutterstock
95. Publisher's collection and Library of Congress, LC-DIG-ggbain-16090
96. Publisher's collection and (photo) Library of Congress, LC-USZ62-133019
99. Library of Congress, LC-DIG-stereo-1s04278 and publisher's collection
100. Publisher's collection
101. Wellcome Library, London